This book should be returned to any branch of the
Lancashire County Library on or before the date shown

Lancashire County Library
Bowran Street
Preston PR1 2UX

Lancashire
County Council

www.lancashire.gov.uk/libraries

Also by Bobby Cummines:

I Am Not A Gangster: Fixer.
Armed Robber. Hitman. OBE.

THE PARKHURST YEARS

MY TIME LOCKED UP WITH BRITAIN'S MOST NOTORIOUS CRIMINALS

BOBBY CUMMINES

WITH DAVID MEIKLE

EBURY
PRESS

3 5 7 9 10 8 6 4 2

Ebury Press, an imprint of Ebury Publishing
20 Vauxhall Bridge Road
London SW1V 2SA

Ebury Press is part of the Penguin Random House group

Robe ntified
h
8

www.penguin.co.uk

A CIP catalogue record for this book is available from
the British Library

ISBN 9781785035166

Printed and bound in Great Britain by Clays Ltd, St Ives PLC

Penguin Random House is committed
to a sustainable future for our business,
our readers and our planet. This book is
made from Forest Stewardship Council®
certified paper.

I dedicate this book to my wife Ami; my son Kai; my daughter Sophie; and my daughter Abigail, R.I.P.

CONTENTS

A FEW WORDS FROM BOBBY

Just a few words from me to tell you what I've been up to.

I had such an amazing response to my previous book, *I Am Not a Gangster*, that I thought a follow-up was needed.

My co-writer, David Meikle, reminded me that I'd been banged up in Parkhurst at the same time as Reggie Kray, Charlie Richardson and Frankie Fraser as well as scum like the Yorkshire Ripper and a whole lot more. David had also written a book with Charlie Richardson, which had a section about me.

David said: 'Who else has a story like that to tell? Sounds like a follow-up to me.'

Hold up a minute, he was right. I could only scratch the surface about Parkhurst and Albany during my previous book.

You'll find – as you read – that Parkhurst really was Britain's Alcatraz, double insulated with the sea flowing around it. You'll also read about my conversations as I remember them with legends in the crime business. Imagine being on the same landing as Reggie Kray and

Charlie Richardson. Their power within the prison system had to be seen to be believed. And I saw it all.

I've gone through my time there carefully, from arriving on the island chained to a screw, to my eventual downgrading when I was sent to a lower security prison – and furthering my education through the Open University.

Some of my new book is brutal. I was a ferocious individual, trapped in a vicious environment.

There's so much to tell you about the people I met, and the grim life inside Britain's Alcatraz. Charlie Richardson showed me how to channel my anger; he told me that education would be my liberation, and how right he was.

Now, as a free man, I have been able to use all of that energy, brought about by frustration and fury. I have managed to help in the rehabilitation of offenders. I am thrilled that my campaign to reduce knife and gun crime has been gaining momentum.

You would hardly expect a former hitman to receive an OBE from the Queen to recognise work with rehabilitating offenders. Of course, I am immensely proud. I am even happier when I hear about someone who has turned his or her back on a life of crime. You have no idea how that makes me feel.

All my love, and please enjoy ...

Bobby xx

FOREWORD

by Professor Dick Hobbs,
Emeritus Professor, University of Essex

Criminal autobiography is a highly popular literary genre, introducing the reader to worlds that most citizens can barely imagine. While the very best of the genre is extremely valuable to scholars of criminal culture, these tales of gangsters, robbers, drug dealers and others also portray an alternative universe for hard-working 'straight-goers' with a fascination for the dark side. The more vivid, stark and detailed these underworld tales are, the deeper the fascination, and the more the reader is faced with the safe but mundane realities of their own nine-to-five world.

These autobiographies are written almost exclusively at the end of a criminal career, after the justice system has flexed its own considerable muscles, and the once successful criminal contemplates the past. Consequently prison is the main focus of the autobiographies of most major criminals who have reflected on their careers at the end of long sentences spent in notorious institutions such as Barlinnie, Durham, Wandsworth and, of course, Parkhurst.

Bobby's previous book, the gripping *I Am Not a Gangster*, delved into his background and tracked his incredible progress towards receiving an OBE. Now he has gone a step further, with some amazing tales garnered on the inside.

Bobby's account of life in Parkhurst is unique, in that he served time with Reggie Kray, Charlie Richardson, Frankie Fraser and so many other notorious household names at the same time. He is able to go into great detail about his impressions of the prisoners, the regime, the screws 'and all that' inside Britain's Alcatraz, as Bobby would say. He lived every day with leading members of the IRA, which makes very interesting reading indeed.

Parkhurst began in 1778 as a military hospital and children's asylum, and by 1838 it was a children's prison transporting 'apprentices' to Australia and New Zealand. By the time Parkhurst became a prison for young men in 1863, it had a reputation for penal brutality. Its harsh regime, which included the use of leg irons, attracted criticism from politicians, the press and Victorian social reformers such as Mary Carpenter.

By the time Bobby Cummines arrived at Parkhurst in 1979, its brutal reputation was well established. It was a high security prison, the end of the line for those who had been given up on by the British criminal justice system. To be fair, Bobby also had a brutal reputation. A London-based professional criminal, he had already served a sentence for manslaughter, but now he had been found guilty of thirteen armed robberies and associated offences.

He was contemplating spending much of his twelve-year sentence in an establishment that had become a byword for everything wrong with the British prison system. He arrived at Parkhurst and entered a human warehouse of the era's notorious gangsters, killers, robbers, terrorists and others in a Victorian institution which was built to house criminal children.

In this book, Bobby charts his Parkhurst career from his trip on the ferry across to the Isle of Wight, a brief but eventful stay in neighbouring Albany prison, and on to the criminal hierarchy of Parkhurst. Here, Bobby encountered the cream of the underworld mixed in with the mad, sad and simply bad. Via his trading skills and violent reputation, he soon gained the trust of the often delusional gangsters of an older generation, as well as the confidence of one notorious villain who was to prove instrumental in identifying Bobby Cummines's non-criminal potential – and encouraged him to take up education.

Along the way, Bobby brokered a deal between Parkhurst's two main factions, and negotiated with 'good screws, bad screws, druggy screws and boozy screws' on an everyday basis. He is also frank about the impact of imprisonment, not just on himself, but on his loved ones.

This book is a portrait of a very different era in British penal history. When Bobby arrived at Parkhurst in the late seventies, the British prison population was approximately 40,000. In 2016 the figure stands at over 95,000, the biggest in Western Europe. Despite a decline in official crime rates, we have clearly become a more punitive society and it is a lot easier get a prison sentence now than it was back then.

Further, drug markets now dominate many prison regimes; prisoners convicted of terrorism are a very different inmate from the Irishmen that Bobby encountered in Parkhurst; and black and Asian prisoners are now disproportionately present in the overall prison population. The working-class neighbourhoods that produced Bobby and so many of his fellow Parkhurst inmates have been destroyed or changed beyond recognition. The unwritten protocols of criminal behaviour are now little more than a nostalgic fantasy, having been erased from all but the keenest memories. Even Parkhurst prison is no more, and along with Albany, is now one of the two prisons that constitute Her Majesty's Prison Isle of Wight.

It is important to stress that prison did not 'reform' Bobby Cummines; indeed, his status as an extremely dangerous man was, if anything, enhanced by the prison system. However, he made certain decisions to live his life in a way that did not involve violence, and on leaving prison he became a powerful and effective advocate for the rights of ex-offenders. He headed a prominent charity and worked on various government commissions. In 2011 he was awarded an OBE.

As you are about to find out, Bobby achieved all of this despite the grim surroundings of places such as HMP Parkhurst.

CHAPTER ONE
CHAINED IN A CAGE

Reality kicked in as, somewhere along the landing, a cell door slammed shut. I heard an echo, then some keys jangling and a screw barking orders. I looked around my bare cell as a glint of morning sunshine penetrated the dust. Heavy footsteps approached.

A key turned in my lock. I saw two pale blue shirts, black ties, peaked caps and the customary shoulder straps. Two bleak faces peered from under the caps. My wristwatch told me that it had just gone seven o'clock.

'Time to go,' one of them said. 'The prison is in lockdown. We'll sort you out with food later.'

They hadn't told me where I was going, apart from out of Wandsworth. All I knew was that I should prepare for an early start. The jail was in lockdown because of a disturbance in the night; I wasn't part of it for a change. Luckily, I had some snacks in my cell. At the other end, they would feed me straight away.

I assumed that, with my record of manslaughter and armed robberies, I was being sent to a jail matching my credentials. I'd been an armed robber, hitman and all that – so they weren't taking any chances. I expected to be treated like a dog.

The two surly screws led me from my cell to a security van, waiting outside the main block. It was like one of those big white ones you see ferrying prisoners around. The screws went about their business without uttering a word.

They opened the back doors and placed me in a cage. I felt like a great big budgie in there. I was quickly handcuffed to a chain. I had one set of cuffs on me, attached to another handcuff. After that, a chain connected me to a nervous looking prison officer, and we sat about four feet apart on bench seats.

'We're going south,' I guessed.

It was only a guess, as I'd been sent off in every other direction in the past, and none of the high security prisons on the mainland had managed to tame me. Something new on the horizon, in the autumn of 1979? I wondered.

'You're correct about going south,' the screw answered, knowing that people like me ended up in Parkhurst and its brutal brother alongside, Albany. 'Next stop, Southampton.'

He knew exactly where we were going, all right. There could be no other suitable destination on the south coast. We had to be heading for the Isle of Wight, in the middle of the Solent.

I wondered how my new home would compare with Wandsworth, a hell-hole in south-west London. Everything about that monstrosity reeked of cruelty. The place opened as the Surrey House of Correction in 1851 when it stored the national collection of birch and cat-o'-nine-tails.

Ronnie Biggs, who took part in the Great Train Robbery, escaped from Wandsworth in 1965 while he was serving his thirty-year sentence. Two years later, Biggs fled to Brazil. Wandsworth was also the home of the 'cold meat shed', later to become a rest room for staff, near the end of 'A' wing. That's where all the executions used to take place. I stayed well away from there.

I spent more time thinking about my current situation and what lay in front of me. I looked at the screw and he looked at me. He was a muscular, fit guy with fair, receding hair and an oversized nose. I'd say he was about thirty to thirty-five. I tried to look him in the eye and not at the nose.

I was slim, five-foot-six, with a shock of blond hair and blue eyes. When I was younger, people said I looked like 'The Milky Bar Kid' on the TV adverts. There was more fat on a greasy chip, but in any confrontation between us I would have destroyed him. I was Islington Boys' Boxing Champion at bantamweight when I was fourteen. I never lost a fight.

There was quite a contrast in uniforms, with blue the colour of the day! The screw was dressed as normal with a blue shirt and dark tie, while I had on the Wandsworth outfit. I wore blue jeans, blue jacket, striped blue shirt and slip-on black shoes. You had to have the top button done up in Wandsworth, but I undid it in the van. Who cared?

'A lot of security just for me,' I said, as the van ploughed on towards Southampton, guarded by police cars at the front and rear. 'Then again I'm high security Category "A". They ain't going to do any favours for Cat A people.'

There was no response from the screw, who was probably still sizing me up and felt no need to answer. I did think that the flashing blue lights and the convoy seemed a bit over the top. After all, I was completely immobilised and at the mercy of my captors.

I closed my eyes for half an hour or so. I tried to imagine what it would be like, banged up for twelve long years. I assumed that my rebellious nature wouldn't earn much remission. I had hardly seen any daylight since my arrest, with time on remand, a gruelling court case and then imprisonment up at Wandsworth. Would they put me in solitary on the Isle of Wight? I half dozed off and wondered what the rest of the day would bring.

My arrest had been dramatic, to say the least. I was due to collect a couple of hand guns, with my eldest brother, Freddy, to use on a 'bit of work' – a job. It was a peaceful Sunday morning in the summer of 1978 with trees rustling in the breeze, a few cars being washed and not much else happening in the streets of north London. We parked our motor and heard the Bee Gees song, 'Stayin' Alive', floating gently into the street from an open bedroom window. We almost didn't live up to the words in the song.

The scene was played out not far from the Enkel Arms in Holloway, where we planned our business and discussed important matters to do with the firm. Two of us arrived at the contact's house to collect the weapons. I pressed the bell with my usual three rings, then ...

'KEEP YOUR HANDS WHERE WE CAN SEE THEM OR YOU WILL BE SHOT.'

We both froze.

'Lie on the ground. Do not move. I repeat. Do not move.'

This was serious. A formidable array of armed police surrounded us, with sub-machine guns aimed and ready to fire. The Specialist Firearms Command people had us in their sights. Freddy and I were then ordered to put our hands on the bonnet of a big police motor, with lots of blue lights flashing. I did point out that I was wearing a £700 dark blue pinstripe suit, and needed to protect it, but no one paid any attention. We were whisked off to Holloway nick, and they threw more than the book at Bobby Cummines.

They really had the hump with me. I faced thirteen counts of armed robbery, thirteen charges of possessing illegal firearms and thirteen of endangering life.

Amazingly, there were thirteen of us in the dock; people in my firm were accused of different levels of involvement. Unlucky thirteen or what! I was also charged with fourteen counts of conspiracy.

In a separate case, a couple of years earlier, they had tried to get me for theft, kidnap, intimidation, threatening life and even stealing the Japanese Instrument of Surrender. The story went that a cleaner stole the priceless document from the Japanese embassy in London, and sold it on. I was supposed to have kidnapped the new 'owner' and made a sale to the American mafia.

'I ain't guilty,' I told the judge and jury, and they could see there was no way I could be found culpable. The evidence just wasn't there, so I was acquitted. The Old Bill hated that verdict. My solicitor said I should disappear overseas for a bit because they would nick me sooner or later for something else.

Also, in a previous case in the early seventies, I'd been charged with murder, although that was reduced to manslaughter, and I'd served the seven-year sentence. What happened was this: we knew that a large amount of wages, maybe £40,000, was being stored in a house. We looked for the cash and tied up the people while we did that. One of our guns went off accidentally, causing panic. I had put the gags on, but one was tied too tightly. One of the group choked on vomit and died. The thought of that death on a bit of work haunts me to this day.

To start with, they sent me to Aylesbury Young Offenders' Institution and then I was packed off to Maidstone prison at the age of twenty-one.

This latest set of thirteen armed robberies, five years after release for the manslaughter, meant that I was too dangerous to send to any old low security prison. I would have to be cut off from civilisation and kept under guard in a place where there was no chance of escape. I felt like public enemy number one during the court case at the Old Bailey.

A few days into the trial, I studied my friends in the dock and their families in the public gallery. My pals had been loyal and the families were devoted to their men. To be fair, I was the ringleader; I was the guv'nor. I persuaded the others to plead guilty, go for reduced sentences and take it from there. In short, I decided to carry the can.

As the prosecution and defence teams sharpened their pencils, I stood up and addressed the judge: 'I am guilty of all of these offences. It would be wrong for the victims of these crimes to have to recount and relive their painful experiences.'

The judge's words kept ringing in my ears: 'These crimes are of the most serious nature and deserve to be treated as such. You were no doubt the gang leader and the organiser. During this trial, all I have heard is the name "Bobby Cummines", and yet there are twelve other accused in the dock with you.

'I have taken into account that you changed your plea to guilty to save the victims having to relive those terrible events, and I believe that there is some humanity in you. I will reflect this in my sentencing. I will not give you the sentence I was going to give you. I will reduce it to twelve years. Take him down.'

Although the sentence was lighter than I'd been expecting, I kept thinking about those three words, 'take him down', and the power that the judge had over me. I also wondered if he'd been planning to give me thirty years of bird, until he heard about my gentler side! Other members of the firm received much shorter sentences, and I was pleased about that.

My brother Freddy received eighteen months. He was sometimes called Smokie, because he'd been a fireman and was badly burned in a blaze at Smithfield meat market. They retired him off and he played a minor role with us. My other brother, Frankie, was more an 'up front' gunman and went down for five years. He was brilliant with motors and looked after all our getaway cars.

It was me who got those two into crime, really. During that brief boxing career, when I was much younger, I got involved with some dodgy people. I took over a debt-collecting business because, when I collected £50, I received a tenner. Later, I discovered that the people who hired me got a lot more commission – so I bashed them up and took over their business!

My other brother, Jack, was a complete straightgoer and even wanted to be a politician, so he never became involved in our activities.

I had no regrets about what I had done apart, of course, from the death during that earlier ill-fated robbery in the early seventies when I tied the gag too tightly. I was able to justify everything else as business. I wasn't going out robbing sweet shops or old ladies; I had been a proper armed robber, taking mainly from the banks who were dodgy, anyway, in most people's eyes.

When you're 'bang at it', you believe you won't be caught. You feel invincible. I walked across several lanes of traffic on Holloway Road with my shotgun, nicknamed Kennedy, in my hand, feeling that I owned the place and no one could touch me. I put on a crash helmet, ready to do some business. I put on that crash helmet many times, always believing that I would escape from the Old Bill.

We named Kennedy after the assassinated American president. It had been a .410 bore shotgun – that was the bore of the barrel – ideal for taking out birds or rabbits. The butt had been replaced with a pistol grip. Kennedy was easy to hide under a coat. Anyone facing those double hammers and two triggers would shit themselves with fear.

I told people who lived in my street that I had a job in the city. I gave them the impression that I was well paid, kind and polite. They had no idea about my dark, sinister side.

We used to plan our business in a café. Getaway drivers knew their exact jobs. A lead gunman played a key role along with the bag man who scooped up the cash.

As I sat there, eyes closed and chained to the screw in the back of the prison van, I reflected on how my actions had affected close family. As my dad, Fred, had passed away, I was left with my mum, whose name was Mary, three brothers and four sisters. In terms of seniority my siblings, with a three-year gap in between each of them, were: Eileen, Fred junior, Patsy, Pauline, Jack, Frankie, Vera and then me, tagging along at the end on 23 November 1951.

My dad suspected me of being up to no good in the early days, and knew what would eventually come my way. I wondered how he would have reacted to all this. In the back of the van, I bowed my head for a few moments and recalled the last time I had seen him, dying in a hospital bed from a brain tumour. It was just before my latest arrest. Frankie and I had donned hospital gowns and made it known to a nurse that we were armed. We weren't with him during his final hours; Mum arrived at his bedside while we were being hunted down by the Old Bill.

My life of crime was all beyond her understanding. I vowed to think of ways to ease her pain, but knew that would be tricky to say the least. She was heartbroken when I went down for the thirteen armed robberies. There was so much that she didn't know; I had no intention of filling her in about so many other crimes in my early years. Hearing about the gruesome details in the court case was more than enough for her to handle.

I continued to spend some time thinking that, here I was, facing a long stretch while still in my late twenties.

I'd already languished in the cells at Holloway nick, then several months on remand at Brixton, before being transferred to Wandsworth.

So many thoughts came to me all at once. I wondered: how would I react to being cooped up in a high security prison, cut off from the mainland? Who would I meet in there? Had I ruined my entire future with such a long list of offences? Would my life be in danger?

I only caught a slight glimpse of the ferry through the dark, dark windows. I was surprised at the size of the ship. I imagined a small thing like a tug, churning across the Solent to the Isle of Wight. We drove along a quay and I could just make out the ship's name, *Cowes Castle*.

After a few more pleasantries with the screw in the cage, I could feel the wheels boarding a ramp. It could only mean we were entering the hold. All I could see, with the van's interior lights, were the screw and the chain that kept us together. The driver could get out and have a cup of tea, but we would be in there all the time. The screw was becoming less nervous and more talkative.

'It takes about an hour, out on Southampton Water and across the Solent. It's just over ten miles.'

'Oh right, I didn't realise it was that far,' I said, trying to settle down on the hard bench seat for the voyage.

'You must be a really bad bastard to be in here with this sort of security. They say you're Britain's most dangerous man. That's what they were telling me at Wandsworth.'

'Well, I've done what I've done. I have been a bad bastard. I don't want to talk too much about it. What's your name?'

'My name's Pete. I travel backwards and forwards in these vans. I'm just an ordinary warder. I'm not always chained to people like this!'

After a few minutes' silence I reflected on this bizarre scenario. There I was, talking human being to human being, in the bottom of a ferry perched precariously on top of the waves. It was a little bit choppy, and I could feel the van tilting slightly.

'Tell you something,' I said. 'We're on the water now. If this boat sinks, you're coming down with me. We're going to face our maker. All the others will jump off this boat, but you'll go down with me because I'm chained to you. Can you imagine the driver coming into the back and trying to free us with the water coming in?'

'Yeah, you're right,' the screw answered, staring at me with unblinking, bright blue eyes, set above his large beak.

'Have you got a wife and kids, Pete?' I ventured, trying to keep the conversation going.

'Yeah, I've got a wife and two small kids.'

'Think about it. Think how precious they are to you, and how vulnerable we are. We might as well be on the

12

fucking moon because the rest of the world doesn't exist. There's only us here on this Earth.'

'I've never looked at it like that before, but I can see what you mean,' Pete answered, glancing nervously around the spartan cage.

'We're totally alone. It's just us, in this cage, at the bottom of a boat.'

We both stared around the cage for a few minutes, taking in what I had just said. I didn't feel comfortable, and neither did Pete as the van lurched to the side. He had probably crossed the Solent a hundred times without thinking about it too much.

The screw took a deep breath and changed the subject: 'Bobby, I was wondering. How did this all start? When you were a kid?'

'Well, I did everything they said apart from possessing a razor. I was about sixteen and I'd just started work as a shipping clerk. I saw two plainclothes coppers lecturing some kids in Finsbury Park. Someone had fired a starting pistol, but I could see the kids didn't have one. I told the Old Bill they were dealing with underage people and they should be talking to the parents or someone responsible.'

'What happened next?' Pete asked, his fair eyebrows raised by a good inch.

'Well, one of the coppers came over to me and said I was a bit flash. They went off and came back. One of them pointed to a cutthroat razor on the ground. They said I was nicked and carted me off. Everything else in

13

the prison reports about me is true – but not that. My dad made me plead guilty because it was only going to be a ten-shilling fine. The coppers told him I'd be sent to borstal if I pleaded not guilty.'

I had Pete's full attention now.

'I lost the job, my family ... I lost everything. So those coppers are responsible for that and everything else in my life now. My dad thought he was doing the right thing, telling me to plead guilty. I was fitted up, and it changed me into what I am. A bad bastard.'

'I believe you,' Pctc nodded.

He really did believe me. I could sense a touch of emotion as he realised what had happened all those years ago. I had done some horrible things, though, and wasn't looking for sympathy. An armed robber who's worked as a hitman isn't looking for sympathy.

I thought it was best not to tell Pete about my time as a hitman. So many deaths, made to look like accidents, were hardly talking points on the way to jail, deep in the hold of a ferry.

Pete kept quiet for a while as I stared at the van floor and continued to ponder over my future years behind bars. I could feel the ferry slowing down as it approached Cowes harbour. Next destination: Parkhurst or Albany and, hopefully, something decent to eat.

'You're not going up to the big house yet,' Pete announced, breaking the silence with a well-used name for Parkhurst. 'First stop is Albany. The guys in there are just as bad. They'll probably move you between the two so that you don't get too settled. You'll find it tough – it's a different world.'

He didn't need to tell me. I was ready for anything.

'You do what you do in your world,' I told him, 'and I do what I do in my mine. The difference is that you go home every night to your wife and kids. I don't have a wife and kids. If people get close to me, there's a weak link in my chain. I can't have a weak link. If I feel anything for anybody, I have to cut if off. My lifestyle doesn't humanise people; it brutalises them.'

'Understood,' was all Pete said.

I felt the wheels trundle out of the hold and onto a road. I could see some smart-looking houses, more greenery than I was used to in the cluttered London streets, then a sign for St Mary's Hospital. After twenty minutes or so I caught sight of a sign for Parkhurst Road. We had to be close.

I grimaced as, out of the tiny darkened windows, a set of enormous wooden gates, surrounded by concrete, came into view. Beyond that grim entrance I could just see a set of equally formidable steel gates. I used to watch those Hammer Horror films, and I thought maybe I was approaching something like Dracula's Castle.

For a few seconds, I felt really downcast, thinking about the people trapped in there. This looked like some sort of barbaric fortress. I peered out of the windows again. A couple of screws were doing some searching and tidying up outside.

It was as if the ugly entrance was glaring at me and promising some really bad times. It was like returning to a darker age, when life was cheap and the authorities of the day ruled with an iron fist. I just got a sense of pain and misery as I stared at this blot on the landscape. All I could imagine was some sort of evil torture chamber. I guessed the building was only a couple of hundred years old; perhaps Parkhurst carried on a tradition of cruelty dating back much longer than that.

Somehow, I was transported back to Napoleonic times. I'd been reading a book about the French Revolution in Wandsworth and this place fitted in with the savagery of that period, when gruesome punishments and endless cruelty were the order of the day.

Pete hadn't stopped me standing up for a better look; I appreciated his gesture.

I had a mild sense of relief as we drove on a few yards to Albany. I could tell at once that Albany was light years ahead of Parkhurst. It was modern, like an office block or a building on an industrial estate. It could even have been a tyre-fitting centre. I could see a long rectangular building with regular sets of windows behind a sign on the grass outside. The sign announced that I was entering 'HM Prison Albany'.

As soon as we went through the first gate, we came across other gates. And I could see that everything was electronic. I was surrounded by barbed wire and cameras. The outside of the building had deceived me.

I noticed loads of formidable-looking fences all over the place.

'Good luck, then, Bobby,' Pete said as we were unlocked and separated by a huddle of screws. 'Watch your back. There are some evil blokes in there. I delivered some of them myself!'

'I always watch my back,' I assured him. 'I'll get through this and I'll be a free man again. You wait and see.'

With a burly, muscular screw on either side of me, I was taken to a white-painted office along with three boxes of my possessions. It looked like an area for secretaries with a couple of typewriters, two or three lamps and some filing cabinets. I could see that my boxes were neatly marked on the outside, describing the contents. They must have had word from Wandsworth about my need for food. A steaming plate of stew and veg was waiting for me. I decided to fight the hunger pangs and take the grub back to my cell.

The two screws looked remarkably similar. They were both about six feet, with the standard blue shirts, caps, black ties, black trousers and black boots. One had dark sideburns and a moustache, while the other had the sideburns without the moustache. They both had an intimidating look, staring at me from under the peaks of their caps. They took down all my details, gave me a strip search and led me to a shower room, adjoining their office. They made sure I had nothing hidden anywhere. I didn't feel embarrassed; this was a common routine.

I just concentrated on what had to be done and more or less ignored the screws. We had zero in common.

I was given a box containing my basic essentials and led along a neat, soulless corridor illuminated with strip lighting. I took my brunch with me.

After fifty yards or so the screws stopped outside a small cell. They opened the door and I stepped inside. It measured twelve feet by six or something like that. There was lino on the floor, a table and a basic single bed. It was more of a base with a cheap mattress on top, really. The screws handed me a key to the cell, showed me quickly how to use it, and prepared to head back to their office.

'Everything is electronic,' the screw with the sideburns told me. 'You can't get out with the key. It's just to let you lock the cell when you're in the canteen or the loo in case anyone comes in to pinch anything.'

The window had bars, but it actually looked like a window and not like those tiny ones you see in ancient prisons. I gazed outside onto a concrete exercise yard. There were no shrubs, blades of grass, flowers or anything like that.

I finished the food, which was reasonable, sat on the bed for a while and realised that I needed to pee. In older prisons you had to do it in a bucket and 'slop out' at regular intervals. Here, I could see an intercom on the wall.

'I need to go to the loo,' I said as I pressed the button. 'I'm bursting.'

My cell door swung open inwards and I walked out to look for the toilet. I found it only a few yards away. At first sight this seemed a more liberal regime, although I was going nowhere and just moving around inside the prison.

Cameras on the walls followed me to the loo and back. Surrounded by all of that security, I didn't bother with the key. I'd noticed that the showers were beside the loo. I collected my towel and soap, made the short trip again and felt about ten times better after a fierce rinsing with hot water. One of my earlier escorts arrived with a couple of my boxes containing clothes, books and my priceless white Bush transistor radio with a big dial on the front. I assumed they had searched through everything.

After a restless night and an early start I decided to have a short nap before exploring the place. I wanted to find out what the food was like, what the other prisoners were like, and all about the screws.

I also wondered: how long would they keep me here? Would I be dumped in the Parkhurst torture chamber? What would they do to stop me establishing roots and connections on the island?

The late afternoon sunshine filled my cell with warmth. Somehow, despite the misery of confinement, I felt a sense of hope, brought on by those natural rays.

I drifted off into a welcome sleep.

CHAPTER TWO

THE ELECTRONIC PRISON

'TEA TIME,' the tannoy blared.

I woke up, forgetting where I was. My mind had drifted back to childhood days, scrapping in the streets around King's Cross with my young pals in the fifties. Old mates like Maltese Tony, Tony the Greek and Silly Billy flooded my head; our childhood adventures in streets filled with craters kept my memory bank busy.

For a couple of hours, I'd dreamed of splashing through the craters, remains of the Second World War, in a home-made cart. We found a dead cat and decided to settle a score with a mean chip-shop owner who short-changed us on portions. I threw the mound of gunge into the shop, and it bounced on the counter – straight into the fryer. We never heard the end of that one. Polish Pat, who ran the chip shop, even arrived on our doorstep for a stand-up row with Dad about it. Polish Pat came off second best, although I was reprimanded as well.

Memories of those happier days lightened my mood as the tinny tannoy repeated its message. I returned to the late seventies with a jolt, still getting through that first day. Reality kicked in. My cell door swung inwards again, operated by remote control. I grabbed my key from the table. Again, I thought it was pointless using it because the locks were controlled by a guard, watching a camera. Maybe the key was designed to give me a feeling of independence. The guy in the control room held the real key.

I needed a weapon. I found a tin of milk in one of my boxes, and then jumped on it until the lid gave way, cleaning up the spillage with an old rag. I had no idea who I would meet; maybe someone from years ago would still bear a grudge. I could even face members of other gangs with a score to settle. I folded the lid until it became like a serrated edge. I kept the razor-sharp metal well hidden inside my trousers.

I couldn't see many screws around. In previous prisons, a warder would come along, unlock the door and say 'dinner time' or whatever. Now I appeared to have entered the electronic prison age.

My cell was one of six or seven, branching off in a spur. I could see several spurs, all controlled and monitored from a central office. I walked along a corridor for a few yards and arrived at a large dining room. I could see row of tables and red plastic chairs, with around twenty prisoners tucking in. A couple of chaps – our

name for heavy-duty, respected prisoners – were negotiating with the screws on hotplate duty. I was really
hoping for some decent food; I knew, from previous
experience, that it could be okay, then horrible, all in
one day.

I recognised a few faces – the underworld name for
well-known criminals – and that put me at ease. When
you go inside, it's as if you are part of a close-knit family.
They make sure you have your teabags, enough tobacco
and anything else you need. You might encounter people
from firms in north, south, east London or wherever. It
makes no difference. You'll have met them in clubs and
pubs. Inside, they all look after each other.

I heard a couple of people being ultra-polite, wishing
one of the other prisoners a good evening. As in all
prisons, everyone in Albany said 'good morning' without
fail. And everyone said 'goodnight'. The 'p' in prison
stands for paranoia. If you're not pleasant to people, they
think you are plotting against them. Before you know it,
you could get one in the back.

I hadn't seen Eddy Watkins for years. I'd bumped into
him occasionally on the outside, although we'd never been
on the same bits of work. Now, as I stood behind Eddy in
the queue, I couldn't fail to recognise him. He was around
five-foot-six, with shoulder-length mousey-brown hair.
He was also known as 'Teddy Bear'. He wasn't that
cuddly, though, because he was the first person to be
convicted of killing a customs officer in 200 years.

We shook hands at once, with Eddy giving instant information. 'If there's tension or any trouble, they only let in six at a time for the meals. It all depends if things are kicking off.'

I could actually detect a lot of tension in the air. I'd never experienced anything like it. I felt as if something was about to happen; I've no idea why, but I could just sense trouble, and it was still my first day in Albany.

I collected the necessary cutlery as I progressed along the queue and held out my plate. I could see they were keen to fill me up with bread, chips and pies. Eddy had similar helpings, but with an even higher mound of bread. I spotted a couple of chairs near the hotplate and we sat down together.

'You can take it back to your cell if you want,' my pal said, attacking the hard-looking pastry. 'If there's too much tension, that's what I do.'

'I'm happy enough sitting here. I read all about you in the papers. It was on the front pages.'

Eddy confirmed that his job had been a total disaster. He told me that customs people were interested in a shipping container in a commercial garage, down at Fareham near Portsmouth. Eddy owned a car-repair business. However, the container was receiving most of the attention from his workers while the car-servicing side had to take a back seat.

'We were fitting it with a false bottom. The coppers were just as interested as the customs people. I didn't know they were spying on us.'

Eddy explained how all eyes, criminal and legit, were fixed on the container as it headed for the docks on a truck, bound for Pakistan. The steel hulk reappeared back in Britain at Felixstowe with a cargo of shoes and a freight company removed the legal load.

But around £1 million worth of cannabis was packed, undetected, in the false bottom of the container. Eddy arrived in a lorry, loaded the container on board, and drove off with his valuable haul.

The customs men and coppers kept their distance and watched as Eddy pointed his lorry in the direction of London. The coppers were armed, but there were issues with using firearms on their home turf, so this criminal wasn't going be whacked.

'I was getting nervous,' Eddy told me. 'I felt as if I was being followed. I wasn't sure whether it was the Old Bill, customs geezers or whoever. I even thought it might be another firm trying to rob me. I drove into the East End. I stopped at a few phone boxes to see if I could find a safe house and dispose of the gear. The customs men must have seen all of that.'

The undercover Old Bill and the customs officers decided to make their move. Eddy recalled that he stopped in Commercial Road to make yet another phone call. One of the coppers, along with customs man Peter Bennett, confronted him. Eddy became as dangerous as a cornered, wounded animal.

The copper produced a set of handcuffs, but Eddy was having none of it and made his own fatal move. Hidden inside his anorak was a 9mm pistol. I was gripped, to say the least, as Eddy described what happened.

BANG! The gun went off and Peter Bennett fell to the ground, dying. The coppers gave chase.

'One of them felled me with a rugby tackle. I kept firing, without hitting anyone, and one of the Old Bill managed get the gun off me. That was it. Game over.'

Although it happened on a job, Eddy had no intention, when he set out, of killing the customs officer. The bloke who died was thirty-two and married with a year-old son. That's how the tragic events panned out on the day.

Eddy received a life sentence for murder with a twenty-five-year recommendation. The operation had been masterminded by Dukie Osbourne, who was very friendly with the Kray twins. He'd just done a long stretch and couldn't face another lengthy spell inside. Eddy said that Dukie committed suicide, with an overdose, in a house on Hackney Marshes.

'The whole crime was cursed,' he told me. 'Everything that could go wrong did go wrong.'

After filling ourselves to the brim with the stodge, Eddy suggested a walk around the outside exercise yard. We strolled along a corridor, and there it was: a big concrete area, about the size of a football pitch. Some prisoners were walking around, one or two had their running gear on and others simply stared into space, no doubt dreaming of life on the outside. I had a good look around to take in the scene. In prison, one thing you lose is sense of distance. You're looking at walls constantly, so the only time you see any real space is when you go out on the exercise yard.

Eddy pointed at a couple of oddballs in the Vulnerable Prisoners Unit, or VPU, and pulled a face. He said the place was full of nonces and grasses; he shared my hatred for them, detesting both groups with equal venom.

As we chatted, the atmosphere was pierced with the high-pitched jangle of alarm bells. Screws ran everywhere, pointing and shouting. I wondered whether someone had tipped over the food trolley or attacked one of the staff.

'It happens all the time,' Eddy assured me. 'The chaps just do it to wind them up. It can be like the Keystone Cops in here sometimes.'

Within seconds the racket had died down. The screws stopped running around, the tension in the atmosphere seemed to ease a little, and I relaxed.

'False alarm,' a voice echoed over a tannoy, from somewhere deep in the bowels of Albany.

The screws were due to 'bang up', or make sure we were in our cells, at nine o'clock. I drifted back earlier with Eddy. It had been a long, eventful day.

Passing the TV areas as I returned, I could see separate sections for ITV and BBC. Up to twenty people could watch the telly in each room. Some of the grim expressions looked far from friendly.

'It's dangerous in there,' my friend warned. 'One feller boiled up some milk the other day and poured it over someone's head. The guy was just watching telly. There was sugar in it and the stuff stuck to his skin. He was in the hospital for ages. You have to be careful not to sit in someone's chair. It can kick off big time after that. The seats at the front are all spoken for.'

After saying goodnight to Eddy, I returned to my cell and switched on the radio. At nine o'clock on the dot, the cell door swung shut with a sharp buzz. I listened quietly to music for a couple of hours, then put the speaker to my ear and tuned in to *Book at Bedtime* on Radio 4. That was my usual entertainment. I learned all about authors, the latest books and any material that I should be reading.

By this time I was dog tired. The first night in a new prison is the worst of all. You never know what the next day holds; whether someone will whack you, who you'll meet and how you'll settle in.

Despite my kip in the afternoon, I drifted off into a deep, deep sleep. During my active years, I'd slept with a gun under my pillow. Lying on the flimsy mattress, I kept that sharp tin top within easy reach.

I had entered a jungle full of dangerous lions and ruthless predators. I was determined to survive.

CHAPTER THREE

MAYHEM ON THE ISLAND

The rising sun filled my cell with welcome, dazzling rays. A thin mist hung like a shroud outside my window, pierced in places by that surprisingly bright glow of autumn. I wished I could see more of the Isle of Wight and its famous attractions, rather than staring at cell walls.

I checked my watch. Seven o'clock. After catching up with the news headlines on the radio and scanning a couple of books from my box, I was all set for the cell to open at eight o'clock. The door swung open exactly on time. I nipped along to the loo and back again, ready to take on the challenges of the day ahead.

Off I went again down to the canteen. I didn't see Eddy this time. I said hello to a few people in the queue, although I wasn't too sure who they were, and studied the breakfast offerings. I knew that I would get to know everyone in due course.

The porridge didn't look like porridge. A voice in the queue confirmed my suspicions. 'It's Canadian pig meal. Tastes great if you're a pig. They should feed it to the screws.'

I noticed small boxes of cereals, like the ones you get in budget hotels, sitting alongside trays of eggs and bacon. I could tell that it was powdered scrambled egg. I recognised the awful stuff from previous sentences on the mainland. It was all dried up, with bits of powder sprinkled over the top.

I opted for bacon, powdered egg and toast. I grabbed a fork and tried a quick sample. The egg was probably the worst thing I had tasted in any prison. I thought to myself that there must be plenty of hens on the island, so there was no need to buy in rubbish like that.

I headed back to my cell with the gruesome concoction on a tray. When I had finished eating, a tall, untidy beanpole of a screw appeared with a smarter accomplice and led me back to the office. There must have been a change of shift since my arrival and the first welcoming party.

I sat down and the beanpole produced some paperwork in a ring binder. The rings clicked as he opened them and I sat down to listen.

'We're having a look at your record. You've got quite a bit of form with these armed robberies and everything. We're hoping you won't cause any trouble. If you do, the next stop is Parkhurst. It might be like going back in time for you, compared to the facilities here. It's a grim place over there.'

'I know it'll be rough. The boys told me all about it when I was in Wandsworth – Britain's Alcatraz, they called it, because of the sea and all that. I'm sure I'll know a lot of people in there.'

After the beanpole had checked through my records and made sure I agreed with the contents, I made off in the direction of the TV rooms to pass the time. Some of the chaps were watching an old black-and-white film. I remember it was *Dr Strangelove*, a comedy starring Peter Sellers, all about nuclear weapons. I sat at the back so as not to annoy anyone, and watched for a while.

I was perched next to an old, wizened bloke who looked like a pathetic victim of the prison regime.

'What are you here for?' I whispered. 'Name?'

'I'm Trevor. I keep doing bits of work and getting caught. I've caused a lot of trouble in here, too. I just make a nuisance of myself.'

'I've just arrived after making a nuisance of myself on the outside,' I said.

Trevor produced a rusty old roll-up machine, measured out a generous helping of tobacco, fiddled with it for a few seconds and a neatly formed cigarette appeared. He decided to tell me about prison work.

'You'll get about £3 a week for cleaning or whatever they get you to do in here. You use that at the prison shop. You can get newspapers, sweets, orange juice, biscuits and tinned milk. I guess you'll have worked out other uses for milk tins. We all keep the tops for weapons in case anything kicks off.'

Trevor said that some inmates carried out maintenance work or had jobs in the kitchen. Others worked in the hospital wing and a few guys kept the outside tidy. None of that appealed to me.

'I haven't seen that many screws around,' I said, moving the conversation on. 'With all of this electronic stuff, I've seen just a few checking, walking here and there. It's nothing like Wandsworth.'

'They control a lot with their electronics, but when you come across them they are evil,' Trevor hissed. 'They can be a nightmare, as if they're hand-picked to inflict grief and misery on us all. Basically, it's a group of thugs fighting the criminals. The mentality is, "I had a wrestle with Reggie Kray or Charlie Richardson." That's how they look at it.'

'But those two are at Parkhurst,' I corrected Trevor. 'At least that's what I heard, although I know they get sent all over the country and back again to stop them causing too much trouble in one place.'

Trevor confirmed what the screw in the van had told me: 'Some of the chaps spend time at Parkhurst, then a stretch at Albany, then back again. They'll do anything to stop us plotting and scheming. Some of the screws float between the two prisons as well. They do their boasting down the pub to entertain all-comers. They probably ain't got a clue about the Krays, but they give it large anyway.'

He said a few of the hated Albany screws preferred to stay put in their high-tech, brutal surroundings, hardly setting foot in another prison.

'There are two really nasty bastards here. We don't know their names. One has a black beard and black eyes.'

A few minutes later, I caught sight of the bearded one he was talking about. He was stocky, around five-foot-ten with a muscular body indicating that he did weightlifting or a sport like that. His mate was a thickset, fat Jock. I could hear him talking in a strong accent. I have nothing against the Scots generally, but this geezer looked as mean as they came. His expression could only be described as a snarl.

'If you go to either of them for anything, you can rest assured you won't get it,' Trevor said. 'They're beating people up at the punishment block. The boys were complaining about the grub and overturning the food trolley, but they didn't deserve the beatings.'

Trevor told me that several of the Albany screws were ex-Army men, who liked to bring their own form of discipline to the job. They'd been in Northern Ireland, meaning that they were enemies of the IRA for a start.

'When things kick off in Albany, you can't tell who the screws are. If there's a riot they send in what they call the MUFTI squad. They're from different nicks, and tooled up in riot gear.'

I knew about the MUFTI squads from previous experience. MUFTI meant 'Minimum Use of Force Tactical Intervention'. These guys were brought in from places like Durham to take on the people involved in riots.

Those MUFTI teams were used several times. At Hull prison, while I was at Albany, a squad was on hand when a prisoner barricaded himself in his cell and destroyed furniture. On that occasion, he removed the barricade and it all ended peacefully.

At Nottingham, around sixteen officers were faced with a violent demonstration by eleven prisoners. The group, armed with wood and bricks, had barricaded themselves into a TV room. Prisoners had bruises and scratches and two of the squad were slightly hurt.

Trevor was up to speed on the activities of the MUFTI squads. They had black overalls covering their identification marks, and came complete with riot shields, visors and truncheons. For all you knew, it could be a screw from your own wing laying into the prisoners.

Trevor told me that, if there was a riot going on, they would arrive in trucks and steam in among the fires, broken chairs and overturned mattresses. In some cases, people who weren't involved locked themselves in their cells. But the screws would open up the doors and give them a hiding as well, just for good measure.

Those soulless, grim Albany screws gave me plenty to think about. In my world, loyalty and respect meant

34

everything. The beatings were definitely happening, because I saw the bruises. It was as if they were beating me or a member of my family. I was driven by this sense of injustice and bristled with rage for days. If a boot was aimed at one of the chaps it may as well have been aimed at me personally. Any unjustified action like that fired me up, and prepared me to take the law into my own hands. I waited for the opportunity to strike back.

Only a few weeks after I arrived, I happened to spot the wing governor walking along the corridor with some of his staff. I seized my chance, ran over and grabbed hold of him. He was a short guy, about five-foot-six, wearing a grey suit and sporting a little brown beard.

A posse of screws appeared, followed by another bunch, then more and more. I had two choices: let go and give up my ground, or stay with it and make my grievances known to one and all.

The governor shouted and shouted, appealing to be set free, while I hissed in his ear that he was a rat for approving the beatings.

'He's taking me hostage!'

I hadn't reached that stage ... yet. I held him by the shirt and slammed him against the wall of the corridor.

'Don't you know I'm the governor?'

'And I'm fucking violent. And who said I was taking you hostage? You said that, not me.'

The next stage meant that there was no going back. An Irish prisoner stepped forward and slipped a blade into my hand. I felt the ice-cold metal and pressed it against the governor's cheek. I thought to myself: will they ever release me after this?

I pushed my forehead against his, like one of those football headbutts. 'Why have the screws been kicking the shit out of our lads? Tell me and I might let you go.'

He was crying like a baby. The screws surrounded us, waiting for any change in the situation that would allow them to make a move. Everyone stood still. I kept the knife pressed against his cheek; the warders kept their eyes trained on us; a few prisoners stood around, wondering what was going to happen next. I reckoned that, if I let him go, I would be kicked to pieces.

Something just snapped inside me. I had carried out some savage attacks in my life; this one was no different. As I clutched the knife, I stared at the governor and thought about the number of deaths in prisons. A lot of those were caused by body belts, supposedly for restraining, but totally misused. Those thoughts kept my anger spilling over. I was full of energy, backing our boys to the hilt. I have always tackled a cause full on if I believe in it.

Screws and prisoners stood in total silence as I inched along towards my cell, with the governor shaking at the end of the blade. Along the corridor we went, careful step by careful step.

As I approached my cell I kicked the governor up the arse and pushed him as hard as I could. As he sprawled along the corridor, I wedged the cell door shut with a lump of wood, although it was a feeble effort with the electronics and the manpower. It was a token gesture.

I could hear a chatter of voices outside as the prisoners were led back to their cells and the senior staff held a meeting to decide on their next move. The warders did nothing. They just kept guard outside my cell and kept people away.

Rations were slipped in on a tray along with a slopping out bucket. Otherwise, they just left me in a strange sort of solitary. It was the prison's way of beginning the punishment. I just pissed in the bucket and stayed put. The bucket had to cope with a lot – not a pleasant sight.

Three days and three nights later, I heard the buzz of the cell door being opened by the electronic gear. A large gathering of screws came in and marched me along the corridor into the yard where a prison van lay in wait.

Where was I going this time? I was chained to a screw in the back; I'd never seen this geezer before. He didn't appear talkative, and so I said nothing. The van, again in a blaring convoy, left Albany and Parkhurst behind and headed towards the ferry. This time, I had no interest in the name of the ship or any other details. The Solent was even choppier than the previous trip, making the journey over the water fairly uncomfortable.

At the other end, the surroundings took me by surprise. I was in Portsmouth, not Southampton as I'd expected, and on the way to the prison there – HMP

Kingston. As the van entered the yard and I was escorted to my cell, I could see that this was a Victorian monstrosity, light years behind the Albany technology.

I spent a few hours settling in and gathering my thoughts before exercise time came around. I was led to the yard by a group of screws with dogs and watched like a hawk.

That daily routine in the fresh air was a welcome relief from the confined space of the tiny cell, although they tried to ensure that I felt intimidated during my break.

It was to be a twenty-eight-day so-called laydown, in solitary, and it turned out to be a grim time for me.

I wasn't allowed to the canteen or anything like that. Other prisoners queued for their food and had recreation time, but I was stuck in the cell. A plump, bald screw in his mid-forties came round and I wrote out a list of what I wanted from the canteen. He trotted off and collected the items on my shopping list.

When he came back, he told me there had been another riot at Albany just after I left. They set fire to wings and caused real chaos.

'I knew that was going to happen,' I admitted. 'I would have been in the thick of it. It was all about the same thing, when I took the governor hostage – conditions and how the boys were treated.'

'Well twenty of them were charged with mutiny and they got more bird on top,' the plump, friendly screw said. 'You'll get a few months extra, too.'

I knew it would add extra time, but that was standard practice. The sense of injustice about the brutality of the prison system still raged inside me. I knew it would never go away.

I did my homework, asking this friendly screw to tell me more about my temporary home. Kingston was another product of the 1800s, with the familiar grey walls towering into the Portsmouth skyline. It had an imposing clock, more than 250 years old, originally from a local church. The main part of the prison was 'The Centre', where all the wings joined, meaning that the screws could keep an eye on everyone.

A printing shop opened in the seventies, allowing prisoners to produce paperwork for the Prison Service. They churned out letters, forms for visitors and that type of thing. A motorbike shop was a favourite place for enthusiastic inmates. They dismantled and assembled bikes, with qualifications in mechanics on offer. Charities benefited from their work when the bikes were sold.

The bizarre aspect of Kingston was that they had a football team, made up of inmates and screws, playing all their games at home in a local league. The pitch was situated in the prison grounds. The prison XI, Kingston Arrows, and opposing teams had one major problem. Because the goalposts were white, they didn't show up against the surrounding white walls. The Football Association gave special permission for the goalposts to be painted blue – the only colourful posts in the country.

On Christmas Day morning, 1979, the tea boy who brought round provisions knocked on my cell door. He was a young kid, maybe just out of his teens. He had a baby face with an innocent look in his eyes. He obviously wasn't innocent, but he looked out of place in there.

'I've a present for you,' the tea boy said, as a whistling screw unlocked my door. 'It's from Jimmy Ash, IRA.'

I knew it wasn't likely to be a bomb! I was intrigued. I thought to myself that the civilised world was preparing to open presents and have Christmas dinner, and I had nothing ... apart from this offering from the Irish Republican Army.

Receiving that white paper bag meant so much to me. I couldn't wait to have a peek inside. I emptied out the contents: tea bags, tobacco, cigarette papers and soap. I'm a hard man, but that gesture moved me.

I only caught sight of Jimmy Ash once, when he was being taken for his exercise at Kingston. I could just make out his jet-black hair and well-built muscly frame under the lights of the yard. I never knew what Jimmy was in there for. What I did know was that those guys were not to be messed with.

The delivery of my Christmas present hadn't gone unnoticed by the authorities. I heard later through the grapevine that I was marked down as an IRA sympathiser!

You can go into the politics of it all, and say who is right and wrong. When they were doing their military stuff, they were like soldiers; when they went about their everyday business, they were just like anyone else. They gave presents, the same as anyone else, too.

Later on Christmas Day, the screws organised a carol service in the prison chapel. The nonces were in the front row, shaking their tambourines and anything else they could shake. The screws wanted us to sit at the back. I protested along with some IRA guys because it looked like we were second best, with the nonces getting all of the attention. We knew that the governor would want to avoid a riot at all costs. There were visitors in there, who expected to see the service going off without a hitch. The nonces were told to scurry off and we moved to the front while we sang about the Herald Angels at the tops of our voices.

Back in my cell, a group of screws appeared with prison visitors. They were trying to spread the spirit of Christmas and bring me festive greetings. What a load of bollocks. I suppose they were well meaning, telling the Christmas story and all that game, but I was hardly feeling festive. I told them all to fuck off. It was an impossible mission to bring me Christmas greetings.

A couple of hours after the visit, I lay there, having flashbacks about my family, school pals and people close to me. In our world, mums are very important. My mum was a total straightgoer, and in her book everyone was as good as gold. She didn't see bad in people, and even adored me when I was known as the 'baddest man in Britain'. As I drifted in and out of an uncomfortable, restless sleep,

I pictured her outside our house in Bemerton Street near King's Cross wearing her pinafore, handing out sweets to the kids. She believed that everyone had an angel inside them, even though some in our neighbourhood behaved more like the devil.

'Dad's home, he's been fighting again,' she said in my dream. 'Kids, he's been in the wars. Patch him up.'

Sure enough Dad stumbled in the front door, with a fistful of cash after one of his bare-knuckle fights. He disappeared every Sunday lunchtime, only to return with black eyes, thick lips and bruises all over. In my dream, for some reason I saw him fighting, although in reality he made sure that I never saw him boxing on the local green. Again, my mum appeared in the street, shelling peas and drinking bottles of Mackeson Stout. It was all part of the ritual as Sunday dinner was prepared.

Mum was proud to be a cockney through and through, with her roots in Islington and Kentish Town. Her mother was a charlady for a prominent family, and my grandfather on that side of the family was in the Royal Navy during the First World War. My dad's mother was a Romany gypsy with black hair. She was a bit frisky, so they said, when my other grandfather went off to fight in the Boer War in Africa where he won lots of medals.

I had a flashback of Christmas, with fairy lights flickering, and the sharp, pure smell of pine needles. I saw images of my brothers and sisters sitting in front of the log fire, singing bits and pieces of carols. We each had a

Christmas stocking, with pictures of Santa and the elves on them, hanging from the mantelpiece. There wasn't much in the stockings. I remembered getting an orange, some sweets and other bits and bobs inside mine. After the war, in the fifties while there were still food shortages, an apple or an orange were luxury items in a Christmas stocking.

As I tossed and turned I could visualise all of us around the table on the afternoon of Christmas Day. My godfather, Johnny Rattray, was there, singing Christmas carols at the top of his voice. Johnny was an illegal book-maker who profited from the bare-knuckle fights and brought plenty of booze along to the Christmas table.

As we finished eating, everyone fell silent to watch the Queen deliver her speech on our tiny black-and-white TV. It was nothing like today's models. I think it was an EKCO set with a volume button, one for brightness and not much else. Dad had saved up for this state-of-the-art device, and for us it was the focal point of the room – and exciting whenever Dad switched it on.

Dad made us concentrate on every word; insulting the royal family was a serious matter in my dad's world, and he had actually attacked a few people who said bad things about the Queen.

My mum was fascinated by the Queen's clothes, and she took any opportunity to study the Queen Mother's fashions. I was transported back to the Christmas broadcast starting with 'God Save the Queen', followed by the main lady herself doing the speaking. I hoped she would be wearing her crown, but there was no crown in my dream. She was talking about how television would make her message more personal and direct, or something along those lines.

'Happy Christmas,' she wished everyone in the poshest of posh voices.

That was a happy home, and we owned it. My dad was always involved in the building industry. He raised enough cash to buy our house. It was semi-detached with four bedrooms although there were quite a few inhabitants: eight kids, two parents and even an aunt staying there. At least the boys didn't have to share a bedroom with the girls. Things did become tighter for the family because, although Dad had fourteen lorries, he refused to pay tax and was forced to go bankrupt.

My dad had hands like shovels. He was small and stocky, and his party trick was punching the tops off cast iron railings.

He used to line us all up in the front room and say: 'Remember this. You don't bring any trouble to your mother's doorstep.' We weren't allowed to swear and we weren't allowed elbows on the table. You had to ask politely to leave the table and all that.

I had come such a long way, along a rough, rough road, since those early days. Those flashbacks kept coming. Perhaps it was a feeling of guilt because I hadn't lived up to the hopes or expectations of my parents. Possibly the flashbacks were brought on by my predicament and a longing to revisit days gone by. Whatever the reason, I was comforted by vivid pictures in my head of happier times.

But, when I awoke, the ugly reality of solitary confinement kicked in once more. I longed for my wide-awake period to end, so that I could dream the same dreams all over again in my concrete and steel tomb. In the cold light of day, I blanked Christmas from my mind.

Exactly twenty-eight days after my arrival at HMP Kingston, I was back on the ferry to the island. The screw – yet another one – didn't have too much to say this time, either. He looked more like a seafarer than a screw, with his grey hair and wrinkly, weather-beaten face. He wore his full uniform down in the hold; I tried to look as smart as possible with grey trousers and a blue long-sleeved shirt that had escaped creasing.

I was relieved to feel calm, still water beneath the ferry. The choppy journey over to Portsmouth was still etched in my memory and I hadn't been looking forward to a repeat performance. I said nothing; eventually, the old screw broke the silence.

'I can't see you ever going to Albany again after the rumpus you caused,' he said, slowly and deliberately as the ferry churned its way over to the island.

I could see where he was coming from: 'I did get the impression that the Albany governor had the hump with me.'

'Your impression was right. You're going to a real hell-hole now. It's Parkhurst for you, mate. Britain's Alcatraz.'

CHAPTER FOUR

PARKHURST: MY NEW HOME

Again, through the tiny, dingy van windows, I could see the grim wooden gates in the distance. The formidable entrance, surrounded by a huge concrete block, was an unwelcome sight. The sign outside seemed to shout 'HMP Parkhurst'. Driving through the gates, we passed a rusty green iron barrier and arrived outside a rundown reception area with reddish-tinged brickwork.

I had a sense that the place was soaked in pain and misery. I'd been to high-tech Albany, then Kingston from the Victorian era, and now I seemed to be taking a step back into the Dark Ages at Parkhurst.

I was getting used to the routine. A group of warders unlocked me from the chains and handcuffs, and escorted me from the van to a reception room where I was strip-searched and taken for a shower. With nothing found on my body, I was given my small box of essentials such as soap and a toothbrush. They led me upstairs and along the landing of 'B' wing, on the first floor. In mainland prisons, everyone knew that Parkhurst 'B' wing was where they kept dangerous prisoners like me.

I could see two rows of cells stretching into the distance. They led me to a cell near the end. I had a peek inside. It measured around six feet by thirteen. There was a bucket for a loo, a chair and an iron bed with a cheap foam mattress. I could see a tiny barred window, about six inches by four, with a sliding panel for fresh air. The ancient-looking iron cell door came complete with an impenetrable lock. I tore a strip of cardboard from the box and blocked the spy hole.

A screw arrived with another couple of boxes and some letters. Hold up a minute, Christmas had long gone. We were into mid-January but I could see some festive-looking envelopes. I opened them and, sure enough, there were cards from Mum and my brothers and sisters. Mum's card had reindeers on with lots of love and kisses. I was never going to receive those at Kingston after taking a governor hostage. I was thankful for small mercies.

In Parkhurst, I knew that I would be joining the likes of other Category 'A' prisoners such as Reggie Kray, Charlie Richardson and a host of notorious household names. They had received long sentences in the sixties. Now, in 1980, I was joining them at the ripe old age of twenty-eight.

I rummaged around in the boxes. I selected my Sunday best, as always, and emerged for a look along the landing. I was dressed in tailor-made grey trousers and a quality white shirt (could have done with an iron) as well as highly polished black shoes.

I had no time for prison issue black slip-ons because they were low quality and felt like cardboard. I went to the doctor at the first real prison I was sent to, Maidstone, way back in the early seventies, and said I couldn't walk around in them.

'What happened there?' the doctor asked, shocked to see the mess of broken toes.

I didn't need to say anything, really. He could no doubt see the wounds were self-inflicted, bashed by a brick or heavy weight. When I was in a detention centre, only sixteen, I'd decided to break all my toes to avoid running around in the snow, doing press-ups.

I put up with the brutal exercise regime for a month and bashed a few people so they knew I was there. I wasn't going to keep running around fields all day and all that bollocks.

I had to spend a month in hospital with my feet hanging in a cage above my bed. But I enjoyed all the luxuries in there and didn't have to waste my time taking part in exercise routines.

The doctor thought I was nuts and he didn't want to upset me. He wrote out a note giving me exemption from wearing the shoes, and I was allowed to wear what I wanted on my feet from then on. My toes healed well enough, so it was worth going through the pain all those years ago. I avoided the sport routines and could wear my own shoes. Sorted.

Now, at Parkhurst, I could see that we were allowed to walk around during the day. I heard a familiar Scottish voice on the landing. It was an old friend, Ian, chatting quite happily to a screw about rugby. Ian had arrived from the north as a child and grew up in various parts of London. He wasn't a 'face', and liked to keep a low profile.

Ian was around five-foot-six, the same height as me, with dark hair containing grey streaks. He appeared too young, early thirties, to have grey in his hair. He was stocky with quite a stomach on him, gained over the years from his love of fizzy lager. He was never a member of our firm, but I bumped into him occasionally around King's Cross. Ian was a staunch, friendly guy who had carried out a few botched robberies and kept getting caught. He did have a violent past. Those who were staunch supported the other chaps without question, followed everything through to the bitter end, put loyalty as the number-one priority and would literally die for you.

'I heard you might be coming,' Ian said, with a mischievous glint in his eyes. 'This is the only place for you after Albany. We heard all about what happened over there.'

'I don't have any regrets,' I said, firmly. 'I would perform again to make my point.'

'Well, they can expect more trouble at Parkhurst. I see you're suited and booted as usual as if you're going on a bit of work. Excuse my scruffy shorts. Fancy a look round?'

'I'm not doing anything else.'

'A lot of people start off in "A" wing as it's a sort of reception area. "D" wing is quite easy going. You went straight to "B" wing, like me, as that's where they keep the dangerous ones!'

Ian continued with his briefing, pointing out the various buildings: 'So here we are in "B" wing. The ground floor is called the ones, the first floor where we are is called the twos, and the second floor is the threes. They put violent types like us on the middle floor, where we can't dig our way out or go through the roof.'

I knew from experience that prisoners were being moved around all the time, from prison to prison, under the dispersal system. They could be at Leicester one day, Durham a few days after that, then on to Parkhurst or another high security unit. Also, people were moved around inside prisons depending on their behaviour or mental state.

I was laughing: 'What about the really dangerous ones – people they say are more dangerous than us?'

'There's a Special Security Block over there with just a dozen of them. They don't get normal association like us. They're watched twenty-four hours a day. If a serial killer comes in, and they're not sure about him, he'll be kept there away from everyone. The Black Panther is in there. He's the bastard who killed a seventeen-year-old girl. There was some sort of ransom demand because she had a wealthy family.'

I remembered the case, all right. Donald Neilson had been handed four life sentences in 1975 for five murders and loads of post-office robberies. He was the sort of bloke who would have been torn to pieces by the boys on 'B' wing.

'They say he was kitted out all in black when he carried out his post-office robberies,' Ian said, recalling the Panther's infamous crimes. 'You'll know all about him?'

'Yeah, he always wore a black balaclava too. When we were out robbing banks, he was cleaning out the post offices. We had no intention of harming members of the public. That bastard was an evil murderer – and you're telling me he's behind that wall?'

'He is, but you'll be lucky to catch a glimpse of him. It's a prison within a prison. The boys are upset 'cos they believe he can play snooker and go to a gym in there. What did he do to the girl?'

Ian, banged up for so long, wasn't totally up to speed on the case, so I filled him in.

'What happened was: he kidnapped the teenager called Lesley Whittle and demanded a £50,000 ransom. That was back in 1975. He kidnapped her from her home somewhere in Shropshire. He stripped her naked, put a wire noose around her neck, a hood over her head and threw her down a drainage shaft. There was some sort of bungled attempt to pay the ransom. Her brother was late arriving with the money and the whole thing was a complete balls-up. The Old Bill took a lot of grief over it.'

'Naked with a wire noose round her neck? The bastard should be hanged with the wire noose. He wouldn't survive a minute on the wing. I'd like to get hold of him first.'

Still hissing with rage, Ian led me down a cast-iron staircase to the ground floor and out into the open air where we could see several reddish brick buildings, all looking fairly ominous in the misty morning air.

My pal pointed at a grim, anonymous building and screwed up his face. 'That's the hospital or F2, as they call it.'

To me, it looked nothing like a hospital. It had the same red bricks as the rest of the buildings. I could see sash windows behind formidable bars. There were no doors, just escape-proof steel gates. All I could see was a picture of neglect with chips, cracks, faded paint and broken slates. Looking at the place, I realised the importance of staying healthy.

'Who's in there?' I asked, looking at this dilapidated, unwelcoming monstrosity.

'If you need an operation you'll go there, but there's a sinister part of it too.'

'Sinister?'

'Yeah, if people go bonkers and need to be certified, they're treated in there. Who knows if they're really mentally ill? Anyway, Broadmoor is the next step for them. Ron Kray was mentally ill, for sure, and he went to Broadmoor.'

'I've heard some stories about F2,' I said, remembering reading all about it in a tabloid. 'Isn't that the place where they put people in straitjackets?'

'That's the place. I've kept well away.'

'Why is it called F2?'

'F1 is at Brixton. If they think someone is mad, they'll send them there. The chaps call it Fraggle Rock after that kids' TV series about things that look like Muppets. If they're dealing with a really bad psychopath, liable to kill, they would send them to F2 here in Parkhurst. And over there is "C" wing. That's where they keep the real lunatics.'

'Lunatics?'

'Yeah, they're all high as kites over there. You hear about them running around, drugged up to the eyeballs and attacking everyone. They're all mentally ill and can't be controlled apart from high doses of drugs.'

'I'll know now to stay well clear,' I said, taking in what he'd said.

'The whole of "C" wing is run by Dr Cooper. The patients in there are known as Cooper's Troopers. Look over there. You can see some of them. They've got their own exercise yard.'

It was a real motley crew. I watched in amazement as they left the yard, guarded by a group of screws, and headed through the compound, probably to some sort of workshop. I had no idea what work they could do. Several of the group swayed backwards and forwards, no doubt from the effects of their drugs.

Dr Cooper was well known and highly respected throughout the prison system. As well as being the head of psychiatry at Parkhurst, he was the boss of psychiatric services for the Prison Service's South West Region. He was the man who decided if you were insane. He was the man who could have you certified. Fortunately, I was never in need of his services.

'That's the education area, part of "A" wing,' Ian pointed. 'They do basic English, maths, foreign languages, creative writing and stuff like that. There's a library, and if they don't have the book you want, they'll order it.'

'I'll bear that in mind. I'm getting into reading. I'm going to try and learn more and more.'

Ian turned his attention back to part of our wing. 'That's the chokey. I've been in there a couple of times for tipping over the food trolley. I was just fed up of the rubbish grub. It's a fairly standard place as far as punishment blocks go. They've also partitioned off part of "B" wing there and made it into two sections. One part is for punishments and the other is for Rule 43 subversives. The Rule 43 protection lot are there on the left … the nonces and those types that need be kept separated, or they get attacked.'

I knew from experience that Prison Rule 43 allowed for segregation when the prison authorities wanted to maintain good order and discipline. Ian was right in saying that inmates, such as sex offenders and rapists, could ask for segregation for their own protection. The subversives, who spent their lives trying to disrupt the prison system, causing chaos every day, weren't allowed anywhere near the nonces.

'It's pretty basic in the chokey,' Ian said, staring at the bleak exterior of the punishment block attached to 'B' wing.

'I've been to a few and they weren't luxurious,' I agreed.

'Well it must be about thirty yards long and a third of that wide. There are twenty cells, ten on each side. There's a urinal, a slops sink, a shower and not much else. The screws have an office opposite that, and there's a hotplate nearby where they serve up meals. There's not much else to it. That corridor area goes to the strip cells and exercise yard. Well, they're pens, really, like you would keep sheep in. They must only be about eight yards long and half of that wide. All you can do is walk around in a small circle to get some exercise.'

'I'll probably end up in the chokey with my track record,' I told Ian, who was ready with more information.

'The worst thing about the chokey is the slops sink, with the screws watching. I tried to time my needs to fit in with slopping out, but if that didn't happen I had to sit with piss and shit in my pot. Whatever happened I had to walk past the screws with it. They have a lot of screws in there as well. They make you feel like the lowest form of the human race, walking past to slop out.'

So much for the chokey. Ian had more details about my normal surroundings, if I behaved.

'It's similar on "B" wing when you're banged up for the night, apart from having to walk past so many screws. You'll piss or shit in it. In the morning, they'll open your cell, and you'll take the bucket into a big recess in the middle of the landing with a massive ceramic sink in it. You'll tip all of your slop into that and you'll turn a tap to slosh it away. You'll put the bucket back in your cell, but you'll smell it a long way off. The pong is terrible.'

'I've had the same thing in other ancient prisons,' I answered. 'It was horrible.'

'Yeah, here you have all the guys on the wing pouring out their crap, and the stench is unbelievable. When it's time for slopping out, it's as if you are locked in a sewer. It's degrading. People on the end of the wing have to carry the bucket all the way to the sink ... past all the other cells. Some buckets knock against the wall, so you get spillage on the landing.'

I'd seen the spillages many times in other old prisons. The thought of slopping out every morning was hardly appealing, but I knew I would just have to get on with it.

Ian stopped outside the wall of 'B' wing and looked reflective. 'The hard thing for me is the lack of birds. On the outside I was always shagging, and now I'm celibate. Most people in here just wank, but some do go with blokes. They don't know what they're doing half the time cos they're usually high on Valium and puff. There's no shortage of weed in here.'

This was a comprehensive briefing, and I appreciated every word of it. I was happier hearing it from Ian than from someone I didn't know well enough to trust.

'It's the same as anywhere else you've been to, I suppose. There's porn and magazines everywhere. You'll see people doing things in their cells or in the showers. You can easily go into a cell and someone's balls will be deep inside another geezer. A couple of Jocks are that way. There are a few rent boys as well. I've been here a few years, so I'm used to it.'

'If anyone approaches me for sex, I'll cut them to pieces,' I said, meaning every word. 'Everything you're describing, I've seen in other nicks.'

I knew that the attitude towards the homosexuals would be the same as in other prisons. They were usually left to their own devices. The ones who looked really effeminate and acted that way were never welcomed in the company of straight prisoners. There was prejudice against them. Having said that, in the old days, one of our firm – Peter the Poof – was as staunch as they came and we protected him from the jibes.

Some of the gay men I encountered in my prison years were potentially very violent. They built themselves up with weights and could prove handy with a blade. It was wise to stay well clear and leave them to it.

As we went back onto the landing, I recognised Frankie Fraser. The enforcer for the Richardson gang was moved around the prison system constantly. He looked short and wiry, about an inch shorter than me at around five-foot five-inches tall. He had jet-black hair and a rugged look, resembling what we called Red Indians. That was explained by the fact that his grandfather married a native Indian from a tribe in British Columbia in the 1880s.

In my previous prison years, early in the seventies, I'd bumped into Frankie Fraser quite a lot. I'd come across him in Maidstone and a couple of other nicks before the Isle of Wight.

'Hi Bobby, hope you're okay. Just a very short visit, I think. If I'm gone in a day or two, you know I'll be back soon after!'

I grinned and gave him a wave. Frankie gave me the thumbs up. He was talking intently to a screw, so I left them to it.

I thanked Ian and headed off back to my cell with the intention of catching up on some reading. I was still getting to grips with the book about the French Revolution. I'd had it since Wandsworth, read some more in Kingston, and needed to get it finished.

I opened the book and got stuck in. It was ironic, I thought, reading about Napoleon in a building that dated back to his brutal time over the Channel.

I thought more and more about Parkhurst, its grue-some appearance and dangerous inmates. I didn't feel intimidated; I felt that I had the strength to do my bird, make any protests if needed, and sort out anyone who needed sorting out.

And I vowed to improve my education by reading more books and keeping an ear out for anything I could learn from Radio 4.

When freedom eventually came, I wanted to take full advantage and live life to the full – on the outside.

CHAPTER FIVE

ALL TOOLED UP

Every day, I was on guard. Every day, I was tooled up. Anyone could snap at any time. Life was so cheap that every precaution had to be taken.

The TV rooms were risky places, even though it looked as if people were relaxing. The gym, too, had to be avoided if you wanted to stay in one piece. There were cases of prisoners being set upon while lifting weights. A happy mood could change in an instant.

The shower area, down on the ones, was a seriously dangerous place. There were five cubicles, and these were the most hazardous areas of the prison. You would never go down on your own. It was the place where people would be cut or bashed up because they were naked, without weapons handy, and at their most vulnerable.

The attacker would put on a sleeveless jumper, cut out eyeholes and put it over his head. He would be covered up – even his toes – so you didn't know who it was. You were an easy target, standing there in the shower, with your back to the attacker. I made sure that was never going to happen to me.

I used to go in the evenings. We always went two-handed. So it meant that I would go down with someone I could really trust. One of you would have the shower, while the other waited outside with a tool. I always made sure that it was a blade capable of causing substantial damage.

I got out, dried off and took the tool from my protector. It was a case of looking out for someone while they, in turn, did the same for you.

Every prison has its own gruesome collection of home-made weapons, ready for use by desperate men. Most of the lethal implements in Parkhurst and Albany were primitive. Ingenuity meant that high levels of skill were used to make some of the barbaric devices. And you had to keep your wits about you. If you had an enemy in there, it was best to be 'tooled up' at all times, especially if there was friction between the two main firms, the Krays and the Richardsons.

In the education block, you could go on a painting course and make a petrol bomb. They had all sorts of chemicals, and it was easy to make something really nasty with the stuff they used to clean the brushes.

In those days they had flags outside the cells. The flag dropped down if the prisoner pressed a button inside his cell, so the screws knew who wanted something. However, the trick was to tie up the flag with a piece of cotton, and then it didn't drop down. The poor geezer was locked in his cell, and no amount of button pressing would attract attention. I saw a few cases of that. By the time the screws arrived it was usually too late; the cell had been set on fire and he was fried to death. The flag system could also be used to cut someone. By the time the screws got to him and opened the door, the damage was done.

Another potentially lethal method was to get a six-inch nail, hammer it into a spear shape and stick it on the end of a broom handle – or the nail could be hammered flat and sharpened to make a stiletto type of knife for stabbing.

There were quite a few cases of prisoners being blinded. The idea was to put a pillow case or sleeveless jumper over your head, as in the shower attacks. The victim didn't know who was attacking him. Then, the aggressor would throw cleaning fluid into the bloke's face. Ammonia was the favourite because that caused blindness.

If you wanted to cut someone's arse, you used a blade that had been covered in garlic. It was easy; you just ran the metal through a garlic bulb. The wound puffed up and they couldn't put stitches in it. The IRA invented that one, and they showed the chaps how to do it. The blade with the garlic was used to cut any part of the body, although for some reason the backside was a favourite target.

Other methods had a devastating effect on victims. Glass could be ground down and slipped into an inmate's sugar. When digested this slashed the internal organs, causing pain on an unimaginable scale. The geezer would want to die, really, because of the intense pain as his insides bled profusely. I consider myself tough, but seeing that happening tested my emotions to the limit.

The chaps often talked about a gruesome incident involving the Krays. One prisoner, in particular, annoyed the twins. He had to be taught a lesson. This was when both twins were at Parkhurst, before Ronnie went to Broadmoor.

The only weapons they could find were two sauce bottles. They emptied the ketchup out, wrapped the bottles in a towel and broke them. Armed with the bottle tops, sprouting jagged shards of glass, they paced menacingly towards their target's cell door.

Ronnie barged in and sat on the unfortunate prisoner's chest. At once he began slashing away at the immobilised guy's face. Seconds later, Reggie jumped on his legs and started cutting his stomach.

Behind the twins, a 'hanger on' appeared with a home-made spear. He'd taped a bottle top to the end of a broomstick and stabbed the helpless victim with the potentially lethal weapon.

It was a messy job for the prison hospital, with more than tomato sauce to wipe up after that savage attack.

A favourite weapon was a billiard ball or a sturdy PP9 battery in a sock. They could deliver a savage blow. Various bits of furniture also doubled up as coshes. It wasn't unusual for a table leg to be ripped off and used to club someone.

Many new assassination weapons were developed while I was doing my bird. The IRA, for instance, stabbed a prison governor with a sharpened nail, leaving a small puncture hole in his arm. No big thing, you might think; not exactly life threatening. That's what the authorities thought until the governor became very ill within twenty-four hours. The baffled doctors found he was suffering from a bad case of blood poisoning. The blade had been placed in human excrement for seven days before it was used to stab the governor with the intent not to wound him, but to kill him. The plan nearly worked.

Other weapons that could be found in Parkhurst included razor blades melted into plastic toothbrushes. They became cutthroat razors to slash people. Then you had those tops of tin cans folded in half to make serrated slashing weapons – one of the first things I did when I arrived at Albany.

Other people were maimed and blinded by having boiling water or milk, mixed with sugar, thrown in their faces, as Eddy Watkins had described over at Albany. The sugar helped to make the burning mixture cling to the skin. It was a sort of crude napalm, and the results were horrific. If that mixture wasn't available, boiling water on its own could be poured from the urn over someone.

People were stabbed to death over nothing. If you were suspected of nicking an ingredient for someone's dinner, you could be whacked. A dispute over a game of chess could have the same result – death.

What you have to remember is that Britain's Alcatraz was a savage place in the early eighties. Parkhurst and Albany housed the country's most dangerous, sophisticated, professional and prolific killers and assassins. And they taught other prisoners their deadly methods.

Prisoners and screws steered clear of Graham Young, the Teacup Poisoner, and I'll have more on him later. Now, he was a very clever man, and his weapon was poison. We knew that he was capable of delivering a slow, painful death. He could make poison by using moss from the outside of his cell bars. I don't think he even had to dislike you. He just seized any opportunity to see someone gasping for their last breath after innocently enjoying a cuppa.

You could lose your life in a careless, off-guard moment at Parkhurst. Sometimes a prisoner would have to think seriously about taking a rival 'out of the game' for the sake of self-preservation.

I witnessed a typical example in the exercise yard. The IRA were dealing in drugs and the assembled inmates could see a squabble developing over money. One overweight IRA newcomer had murdered a British officer and made it known he was not to be messed with. He thought he was a bit of a Jack the Lad.

I stood there, watching intently, as a highly amusing scene unfolded. Little Joe the Greek was an armed robber, but he didn't just hold up the guards when they stepped out of the van. During his armed robberies, he usually shot anyone who got in his way. Joe wasn't a big bloke but, undeterred by the sheer bulk of the newcomer, pursued him with a blade. A comical chase developed around the prison yard.

'It's like a scene from Benny Hill with just blokes in it,' a voice from the crowd chuckled.

'It's as crazy as the Keystone Cops,' my pal Ian agreed.

'They're off their rockers,' I pitched in.

Joe made a few thrusts in the direction of the newcomer's rear quarters until the screws caught up with them and saved his arse from being used as a dartboard.

Everyone who saw the fracas agreed that the combatants were totally bonkers. Incidents like these simply emphasised, again and again, how you had to watch your back – and even your backside – at all times.

While I was in Parkhurst, I learned about the worst punishment of all. It happened on the outside, apparently, and I heard the chaps discussing it on the landing. Someone would have a tube inserted up his bum. After that, barbed wire would be pushed inside the tube. The tube would be taken away, and the barbed wire ripped out.

Anyone caught with a weapon would expect severe punishment. You could end up down in the chokey with loss of remission and possibly ghosting, being moved suddenly, to another prison. Even if your weapon was used by someone else to cut a rival, you would in trouble too, meaning that care and concealment were vital.

You had to be clever when hiding blades because of the cell searches. There was a chap who specialised in woodwork. I got him to make me a makeshift cabinet with a false bottom, and I kept the blade in there.

My overall impression? There were so many ways of maiming people, and even killing them. Yet, in my mind, the brutal regimes of Parkhurst and Albany were the cruellest weapons of all.

CHAPTER SIX
THE PRISON BANKER

Weapons were essential to stay alive – and cash was vital in the day-to-day running of the prisoners' affairs. Shortly after I arrived at Parkhurst, I used my organisational and 'fixing' abilities to earn a few quid. It was easy and without too much risk, as long as I sorted everything to the letter and left nothing to chance.

Parkhurst needed a banker to manage the prisoners' finances. There were bookies in the nick, although things were a bit haphazard and people could easily get into debt. There needed to be a clear arrangement, controlling the money flow and the prison economy.

I had a good look at the system and decided to make some major changes. Prisoners needed to know there was a lump of money, somewhere, to lend to people – and I was the man to sort it all out. I didn't get any objections from any of the faces; they were happy with an increase in efficiency.

I found a prisoner who didn't get many visitors. I got a bird to write to him, making out she was his girlfriend.

The geezer was a poof, and keen to help for reward. I organised for the so-called girlfriend to bring in £1,000 in £10 notes from contacts, wrapped in clingfilm and stuffed into a condom.

During a typical visit like this, the two conspirators would check how vigilant the screws were. The warders looked out for anything being passed between the people in the room. It might mean a trip to the loo for the bird, the parcel left in there briefly, then a trip to the same cubicle for the prisoner. He would go in and stick the condom up his bum. It all depended on the level of security on the day. That method was also used by others to bring in drugs, although I left that to the dealers and never got involved.

I saw the bum smuggler after the visit and gave him £50 straight away. I destroyed the rest of the evidence, considering where it had been planted, and I counted out my £950. I was in business, ready to start banking and lending.

All of that loot had to be hidden, lively. I went along to an art class in the education area. I was mainly on the lookout for paint, brushes or anything that would be of use to conceal the money. I was hopeless at art, but I nicked the fruit if they were painting apples and oranges. Some people would nick bottles of that paint thinner stuff if they wanted to burn someone out of their cell.

I asked around if anyone went to modelling classes and got them to supply me with putty, white paint or anything they could thieve. With the pickings from my own class, it added up to a nice little arsenal of essential ingredients.

I carefully made a small hole in the wall of the cell with a sharp piece of metal. The hole was close to another one, hiding a six-inch nail that had been hammered down to a stiletto shape for use as a lethal weapon. I used to put the cash in the new hole, fill it up with putty or papier mâché, depending on what was available, and repaint the area with a shaving brush or a small brush from the art class. Papier mâché was best. It could be pushed in and out of the hole in one lump. The used stuff went down the toilet on the wing, to be replaced by some fresh materials.

You could hide weapons, dope or whatever you wanted like that. I actually made a good of job of filling and painting, and was quite pleased with my handiwork!

Every so often I took as much as I needed out of the cash hole, resealed it again and painted it over with the shaving brush. On a typical day I would have £900 in the wall, with £50 on me to hand out as loans.

Everyone got to know that, whether I was at breakfast, dinner, exercise or in my cell, I was the man to see. If people wanted to buy dope, a new radio or even a budgie, they could come to me for the readies at any time.

Normally I charged 25 per cent interest, so that would be a quarter of the money borrowed. That interest could be much higher or lower depending on the person's credit history, background and all that. A close pal might only have to pay back 10 per cent. I made the system easy for people to understand. If they missed a payment, the total kept increasing by 10 per cent and so on.

I made it clear that loans had to be paid back, with no exceptions. Danny, an armed robber from up north, borrowed a tenner to buy some gear. He spent most of his money on drugs. He was in his late thirties, with long curly hair, pink cheeks and a pinkish nose. He looked just over five foot, skinny and undernourished. I wondered how he had the strength to be a bank robber in the first place.

Danny had his date for repayment, a week later at a rate of 25 per cent. He knew that the rate would keep increasing if he failed to pay up. On that day, with the tenner due to be repaid, he came up to me in the breakfast queue.

'Bobby, you know that tenner I owe you?'

'Plus 25 per cent of the tenner, as you know.'

'Bobby, I bought some gear but I owe the dealer too much.'

'That's not good enough. You should give up the drugs. I want surety. Give me your wedding ring.'

'The wedding ring is very precious to me. I can't give it to you.'

'I'm taking the ring. If you don't have my money plus the extra interest in four weeks, it'll go down to scrap gold. I'll keep the money from that instead.'

'I'm not giving you the wedding ring. All I have is my wife on the outside.'

'Then you're going to get fucking hurt.'

'What are you going to do to me?'

'You're going to get bashed up.'

After breakfast there was a knock at my cell door. Danny must have worked out something with the dealer. He had my tenner plus interest. I made it clear to him that, next time, he would have to go elsewhere for his loan.

I explained to people that there were a few ways to pay me back. For a start, they could arrange to get cash from a visitor. I stayed clear of their visiting and smuggling arrangements – that was up to them. They could pay me from their earnings in the prison, or even with soap and teabags.

I didn't want to take all of their money at once, though. I worked out what they needed to live on, gave them maybe four weeks to pay and added on the interest.

If someone borrowed a tenner and wanted to pay me out of their canteen allowance, I would take half of their weekly fiver. They would give me that for the next four weeks to pay off the capital, and then on the fifth week I would get my interest.

If someone was skint they might think about stealing from me, possibly, or try to find ways of not paying. Like Danny, though, everyone knew that wasn't an option.

I bashed up a couple of people myself for non-payment but, with business booming, I recruited an enforcer to help with the workload. He was as mean as they came, and would follow my orders to the letter. Anyone who failed to repay their loan was in danger of a hiding at the hands of a violent lunatic.

'Could you help me out?' I asked Neville the Devil, real name Neville Winn, who was on the same landing as me. I hadn't had a proper chat with him, but thought that this was the time to do business. I was surprised that Neville was allowed to mix with us at all. He was ideal to put the squeeze on someone.

Neville was in Parkhurst for grievous bodily harm. He had scars all over his face, like a map of the London Underground, silvery grey hair and piercing blue eyes. He'd been a minder and enforcer, a role he enjoyed carrying out with the threat of a butcher's boning knife. On the outside, he used to cut people to pieces. He was the man you sent in if someone was taking a liberty with a member of a family, or if a large debt had to be collected. Basically, he was violence on legs. He did a good job on his victims, cutting them to pieces. When he went to work on someone, he really went to town.

Neville was always immaculately dressed, with pressed trousers and an ironed shirt. He polished his cell floor so that you could see your face in it. I don't know why, but he was always washing his hands – maybe it was some sort of compulsive disorder. Everywhere Neville went, screws tried to follow. He was so unstable; everyone in Parkhurst knew he could turn to extreme violence in a split second.

I tried him out when the screws weren't looking: 'Neville, that geezer downstairs owes me a tenner. Could you go and collect it? Do what you have to do, OK?'

'No problem, Luke,' he replied, using my middle name as he preferred to do. That was just something with Neville. If he could find a different way of doing or saying anything, then that was his style.

Nearly every time, he came back with the readies. If he didn't, the bloke who owed the money received a severe beating, or worse, and eventually found ways of repaying my money. Neville was happy with the occasional fiver to compensate for his efforts.

Some of the chaps were afraid of Neville because he was an unpredictable psychopath. I made it clear to Neville that, if he posed any threat to me, then I would have to kill him. He accepted that. We both knew where we stood. I told him that I had a pair of garden shears under my mattress. 'If I ever think you're going to cut me, I'll stab you with these,' I warned, brandishing the rusty old blades.

The other side to Neville was a deep love for his children and his humour. He used to invite me into his cell for a smoke and to look at pictures of his daughter. I was never tempted to try any puff and stuck to roll-up tobacco instead. Neville became emotional as he grasped the colour picture in his hand.

His humour had a dark side. When he was doing his time, he got an eighteen-month sentence on top. He had a row with someone in the nick and cut the prisoner's ear off. When I asked him about his punishment, he said: 'I got an ear and a half!'

It became common knowledge that I would be able to provide an instant tenner, or at least provide the cash in a few hours. A tenner was fairly easy to come by, and so I kept the loans in that range. Sometimes my 'float' all went, and I had to revisit the cell wall for a top-up. People did ask for more than a tenner, but I knew that could lead to problems. They could be borrowing from me to pay someone else they'd borrowed from. All they were doing was paying off a bad debt.

Someone else wanted to buy his wife a jewellery box, made by Fat Fred Sewell, another prisoner. He needed £20, and that was double the normal loan. I needed surety, which had to be worth more than the loan. He gave me his radio in case he defaulted on the arrangement. As it happened, he paid me back on time and everything went as planned.

If anyone wanted to buy drugs or buckets of hooch with the money, that was okay by me. I was in it just for the readies. I mean, when you borrow from the bank, they don't check to find out if you bought drugs with their cash. You just need to pay them back.

One bloke kept missing payments and eventually he owed me £40. I received the money just before he was about to be bashed up by Neville the Devil.

I needed to keep a record of that transaction and everything else that was going on. I knocked at a cell door, down on the ones: 'Gaz, would you mind doing my books?'

I asked Gaz, an older lifer in his late sixties, because I needed someone reliable and who was trusted by the screws. Gaz had been an accountant on the outside. He was always in and out of the wing, into hospital and all that game, so he wasn't under any suspicion.

'Yeah that's fine,' he told me. 'I'll keep a good record.'

'Sorted,' I said.

I hardly needed to say any more. I knew that Gaz would find a pen and some paper, keep my records up-to-date about people owing, payments received and everything else. He also knew that I would make sure he was rewarded. All I did was visit his cell with some basic paperwork.

Gaz reminded me about my ruthless business methods on the outside. 'Ruthless' was the right word: I used to place a £1 note and a bullet on a table if someone wanted to do business with me. A straight deal was the best way, I used to say, pointing to the £1 note. If anyone fucked with me, they would get the bullet.

At Parkhurst, I became a banker and fixer, rolled into one. I had to organise £1,000 for a geezer on the outside to buy some stolen jewellery. I sorted the cash through a contact in my manor. I charged him 10 per cent of the

£1,000 for the day while he got his act together. I was paid pack sharpish because under that deal the rate went up by £100 a day.

'Bobby, I fancy steak and chips tonight,' one of the chaps said, licking his lips in my cell one evening. 'Could you fix it for me?'

'Hold up, I'll see what they've got. I can't promise sirloin – it might have to be rump.'

'I'll go with the rump if it isn't tough. Can I have a glass of decent red wine? You got burgundy last time. Any chance?'

I went down to the kitchen, spotted a prisoner I knew and explained about the dinner request. The main thing was that the provider had to be paid, and I sorted that. A couple of hours later, I was pleased to see a tray arriving in the chap's cell with an impressive-looking dinner. I was paid for taking the risk, and everyone ended up happy.

This was developing into a full-time job. Luckily, I was avoiding my cleaning duties, thanks to a group of eager young boys, so I concentrated on making money. I was considered too dangerous to go to any workshops away from the wing – especially after taking the Albany governor hostage. It all gave me more time to do business. I could arrange anything from delivery of aftershave to the finest whisky, smuggled in from the outside.

Sometimes a prisoner would come up to me and say his kids needed new shoes or a school uniform. I used the same arrangement, organised a contact on the outside to do the business, and staged the payments. I didn't charge interest if the money was for something like that, but the cash had to be paid back. This business on the outside wasn't a big hassle generally, as it was easy to fix. But some issues did arise ...

'Bobby, I've got a problem.'

'A problem?'

I could see Robbie, a middle-aged geezer, standing outside my cell, looking as if he'd been crying. He was trying to appear like a teenager with his football shirt, clinging shorts and branded trainers.

'What's going on, Robbie?'

'I had a message this morning about my bird. It's my wife, as it happens.'

'What's wrong with your bird?' I asked, although I could guess.

'She's being fucked by some geezer in the manor.'

'You're sure?'

'Sure.'

'Name and address?'

Robbie, shaking with emotion, handed me a scribble on a scrap of paper with a name and address on it. That was all I needed. The next morning, I made a phone call. In the evening, I happened to hear that a certain person in my manor had received a severe beating. He survived, unlike his new relationship. That love affair was dead. No charge for Robbie.

I decided to take an important precaution. I had arrangements in place to continue as a banker at other prisons if I was moved out. That plan would mean organising to have £1,000 smuggled into the new prison for me. I would take £250 in cash, hidden on my body somewhere. I would leave £1,000 in Parkhurst for the new banker. The economy of my previous prison and new home would still run smoothly, with a lot of help from the outside. I would only take a cut in the new prison when everything was running smoothly.

I really enjoyed the company of my pal, Ian. One evening, after my day of fixing, we watched the local news programme in a TV room. Fred Dinenage, the newsreader and star of the *How* kids' programme, was introducing a story about the Isle of Wight ferries being disrupted because of the weather. We just shook our heads and both muttered that there would be no visiting for a while in those gales.

Ian asked me about my growing business. 'Bobby, I thought you were a gangster. What's all this business stuff? Were you doing it as a kid?'

I explained that I had an eye for business, even as a young boy – and the inspiration came from my dad, even though he was a straightgoer. When I was a kid, vandals used to break our windows. Dad complained that his insurance premiums kept going up. I didn't have to do much to achieve a steady income. In a roundabout way I chatted to a couple of shopkeepers about the problems of vandalism around King's Cross.

I gave the interested Ian more details: 'I found out that, after two attacks on their premises, insurance premiums rocketed. That third strike cost them a fortune. All I did was to track down the kids who threw stones at shops and restaurants, keeping a careful note of their attacks, and making sure there were just two incidents. The business people knew that a third attack could prove fatal for their trade, so I offered to protect the commercial places from vandals.'

'I can see how that worked,' Ian said after a few seconds, thinking about the pros and cons. 'But some of those places would suss you out, surely?'

'I offered to protect the shops, pubs and restaurants from the bricks. All I did was collect my money and give a percentage to the vandals, and they didn't need to break any more windows. Insurance premiums were kept low and there was hardly any vandalism. A couple of places noticed the drop in crime and said they had no more use for us. Another brick through the window meant that they were back on our books.'

I told Ian that another regular income came from just having a few chats here and there. I made it known that a restaurant's food was terrible, and several people had been poisoned. I paid several kids to tell people in the street.

After a couple of days I could see that the place was empty and the owner looked a worried man. I went inside, said I would make sure the whole area knew the food was good again, and he gave me regular payments. He had no choice. Easy money.

Ian nodded. No doubt wishing he had the skills to operate my schemes, I thought.

The way I saw things in Parkhurst, no one was getting hurt, unless they didn't pay me back. I wasn't dealing in drugs. Everyone could borrow money to enjoy a better lifestyle. I was never caught operating my banking and fixing activities.

I made sure that everything was sorted professionally. I wonder if the screws suspected, and turned a blind eye? I'll never know.

CHAPTER SEVEN

TIME WITH REGGIE KRAY

I recognised the familiar figure straight away. It was someone who had been in the papers for years. The general public were used to seeing him suited and booted; I saw him in black shorts, white vest and a pair of gleaming new trainers.

'I remember the face,' Reggie Kray announced across the landing as I strode up to my cell. 'Where have I seen you before? Refresh my memory?'

'I'm Bobby Cummines. I met you and Ronnie at the Old Bailey when I was sixteen. I was up for using a sawn-off shotgun and armed robbery.'

'Oh yeah?' Reggie said, leaning on the railings.

'It was during your murder trial. I was walking along the landing from the cell to my court. You and Ronnie looked like a million dollars in your suits. You were in Court One, so I knew it was a big case.'

'I remember now. We bumped into you during a tricky time; 1969, it was. We were up for murdering Jack the Hat and George Cornell. That's why we got thirty years.'

'Ronnie called me a cheeky bastard,' I said as I walked up to Reggie and shook his hand. 'He said I had some front, and gave me ten out of ten for that. He said you would be seeing a lot more of me. Well, you will now.'

I knew the story off by heart. Ronnie shot George Cornell in the Blind Beggar pub, Whitechapel, on 9 March 1966. Cornell was an associate of the Richardson gang, and there had been bad blood between them and the Krays. George didn't help himself when he called Ronnie 'a fat poof'. That's what George is supposed to have said, although I wasn't there to hear it. The story goes that 'The Sun Ain't Gonna Shine (Anymore)' played on the jukebox while George fell to the ground with a bullet in his head.

Only twenty-four hours before the Cornell killing, there was a major incident at Mr Smith's club in Catford. Frankie Fraser and Eddie Richardson, Charlie's brother, were injured in a brawl there. Dickie Hart, an associate of the Krays, was shot and killed.

They couldn't pin the killing on Frankie, who was jailed for five years for affray. As it happened, he was still serving the sentence for the Catford case when he received another ten years after the so-called 'Torture Trial' in 1967. Charlie Richardson and his associates were handed long sentences, despite constant denials and protests about lack of evidence.

It's well documented that Jack 'The Hat' McVitie had failed to fulfil a contract to carry out a killing, although he'd received the money. It all happened at a flat in Stoke Newington a year-and-a-half after the Cornell shooting. Ronnie held McVitie in a bear hug while Reggie stabbed him with a carving knife.

'Ronnie was nutted off to Broadmoor. He hated Parkhurst – really hated it here. He played up and made sure he was sent to the nuthouse. We write to each other all the time.'

I was all ears as Reggie stood there on the landing, looking me up and down as he talked.

'Did you know much about us when you went into the court?' Reggie asked, his face screwing up in quizzical fashion. I guessed that Reggie must have been slightly deaf because of the way he turned his head and watched my lips.

'I didn't know much at all. The screw beside me said I'd been talking to the kings of the East End.'

Reggie laughed: 'He was taking the piss. They hated us and we hated them. We were kings of the East End, though.'

I assessed the change in Reggie since that last meeting. Then, at the age of thirty-six, he had strutted around the Old Bailey in a flashy suit, immaculately groomed.

Now, in 1981, I could tell quite a difference. His sharp, chiselled features were set under greying hair. He wasn't the tallest, about five-foot-seven, and he was quite wiry.

It was common knowledge that he'd been a decent boxer, and I could just tell that a well-placed right hander would be a jaw-breaker.

Most of the prisoners walking along the landing just wore casual clothes, in the style of Reggie. That was never my scene.

'This is all I wear,' Reggie explained. 'It gets too hot on the island, even in the spring and autumn. Vests, head-bands, shorts ... look at this lot. I see you haven't reached that stage yet.'

'I've always been the same, Reggie. Ever since I was a young man I felt underdressed if I didn't wear a shirt and trousers. When I was "at it" doing the robberies I wore a three-piece suit. I just saw it as doing business.' I told Reggie that I'd arranged for the laundry to iron my shirts and trousers.

'You're the banker, aren't you? You and Neville the Devil are the smartest people in here,' Reggie grinned. 'He's the ideal man to make sure people repay your loans. He might kill them if they don't! I've seen some crazy people. I've been here more than ten years, so I've seen a few come and go. Have you heard of the bedsprings swallower?'

I had to confess that one had slipped under the radar as far as I was concerned.

'Well, we never really knew his name. He sort of disap-peared to Broadmoor, a bit lively. He was always in the hospital having the bedsprings removed from his stomach.

'We're all glad he's gone. He went a bit crazy and attacked a feller with a brick from the rockery. It was nearly fatal. The feller became a vegetable in the hospital and he was taken off to a special unit somewhere. That was the last we heard of him or the bedsprings swallower. I imagine the oddball must have moved away from Broadmoor because Ron has never mentioned him.'

Reggie gestured towards his cell at the extreme end of the landing. I was three or four cells away on the same side.

'You're a couple of cells away from Charlie Richardson. He's been ghosted off somewhere for ages, but he's just come back. He has a big firm in here. We get on all right most of the time, although Ronnie isn't happy about that. He hates the Richardsons.'

'I'm sure I'll meet Charlie properly soon then,' I said.

Reggie ushered me into his cell. I sat down on a basic wooden chair while he prepared the tea. One of his eager young followers had already gone into the cell and brewed up, placing milk and sugar on the table. Reggie checked inside the pot, and then poured carefully.

I took a good swig as Reggie went into full flow.

Reggie's cell looked fairly comfortable. He had burgundy curtains in there and a fancy matching bedspread. There was another mattress, with a wooden frame around it, made from a chair – so it looked like a half-decent settee.

'People on the outside sort all this out. They bring in bits and pieces and the screws don't seem to mind. Some of the young kids do their bit as well, so it's not too bad.'

'You've crammed a lot in here,' I observed, looking at pictures on his walls. I could see photos of Barbara Windsor, Judy Garland, Shirley Bassey, George Raft and Al Capone.

'Some of them come to see me,' Reggie said proudly. 'Barbara is coming next week. I get lots of letters.'

I had read in the papers that Barbara visited him. She was married to Ronnie Knight, another gangster of our time.

The centrepiece of his cell was a picture of the Queen, about A4 size. She looked so glamorous with her crown and jewels, gazing into Reggie's cell from the all-white paintwork.

'I'm a royalist too,' I told him. 'I've a picture of the Queen in one of my boxes, so I must hang it up. That's a great picture of the Queen Mother as well.'

'The Queen Mum and King George came down the East End during the wartime bombing. You'll know that anyway. They won the hearts of the people. I always have pictures of royalty in my cell.'

I wanted to know more about how his brother Ron had tried to cope with the brutal atmosphere in Parkhurst, and prompted Reg with an inquisitive look.

'Yeah, well Ron was certified as a paranoid schizo-phrenic before he was sent to Broadmoor. This place was really getting to him.'

'Did he manage to keep out of trouble?'

'No way. It was all to do with his medication. I remember one time they were late giving it to him. Ron threw a bit of a wobbler and said he was going to do the bastard. He threw a right hander, sending the screw down on the floor. He broke the screw's jaw, but they only discovered that later. I remember Ron saying: "Can I have my medication now?" It was typical Ron.

'That earned Ron fifty-six days, I think it was, in the chokey. I've done solitary, you've done it too.' Reg obviously knew a lot more about me than he let on to begin with. 'Twenty-three hours a day cooped up in the tiny cell over there was a horrendous experience for Ron. He's much better off at Broadmoor with his own room and everything.'

Reg told me that Ron had undergone electric shock treatment in the hospital at Parkhurst.

'I had a bout of that several years ago,' I told him. 'It was horrible. What happened to Ron?'

'Well, he had two lots of it,' Reg told me. 'They took him up to the hospital and gave him an injection. That made him unconscious. After that they gave him the shocks. He lost his memory for a while but in the end felt a lot better. I think it actually did him good.'

Reg explained that, like Ron, he had also suffered from some sort of paranoia.

'I stopped writing letters, thought I didn't have any friends left, and even stopped shaving. My hair just became a mess. I couldn't be bothered. I was just confused and even imagined I was going to be taken to an airport. It was all a muddle.'

'What happened after that?' I asked, wondering how he had got through all of this.

'I tried to commit suicide at the hospital here. They were trying to find out what was wrong with me. I broke the glass in my specs and tried to slash my wrists. Anyway, I didn't do enough damage and they saved me.'

I assumed they had given Reg drugs to control his illness.

'I got through it just by reading. I read a book about how you had to keep going, whatever happened, and gradually I saw the light. I just changed my mindset and became more positive.'

'How often do you and Ron write to each other?'

'Every day.'

Reggie reached for a plastic bag on his table, opened it and thumbed through a pile of envelopes. He showed me one of the letters. In big writing at the top it said, 'Now hear this!' The writing went up and down in peaks and troughs, like a heart monitor, and it was just down one side of the page. I was surprised that Reggie trusted me so quickly, showing me his personal stuff. I guessed that as he'd met me before and had checked me out, he felt comfortable.

'He calls the letters "Colonel Biffs" for some reason,' Reggie explained. 'He adds the "Now hear this" part if he's annoyed about something. Look, he's saying that someone upset him in the canteen at Broadmoor. He says he confronted a bloke who insulted him while he was having his dinner, although the feud didn't go any further. I hope it doesn't go any further. He can do scary things on his medication. You want to see what they give him, Largactil and that sort of thing. It would knock a horse out.'

I felt sad in that moment. Reggie, hard man of the East End, was hurting without his twin. It was like a child being taken away from its mother.

Beside the pile of letters, I could see that Reggie was writing a reply. I could hardly make out a word. It was just a scribble. I assumed that the two of them, communicating since childhood, would make out what was going on, even if no one else could.

As we talked, a couple of young boys – they were very young – came into the cell and cleared up the tea things. They must have been in their late teens, and wore the same brand of trainers as Reggie. The pair nodded respectfully as they tidied the table.

My impression was that Reggie was in his own little world. He could have gone to any prison with the same result. He came inside with his head, body and soul – all intact and impenetrable. I'd heard lots of rumours about Reggie being gay, but he didn't give me any indication of that.

It seemed to me that the young guys, coming and going, were stargazers. He had them around him all the time, but if it was sexual he kept it all very close to his chest. At that stage, I reckoned Reggie enjoyed the adoration, and people giving him a leg up – that was a phrase we used to give someone a helping hand.

Ronnie, of course, was openly gay and made everyone know he was that way inclined. It was a well-known fact throughout the prison system.

I stood up, thanked Reggie for the tea and prepared to head back to my cell.

I knew that Reg might not be there the next day, with the dispersal system in full flow. He could easily be ghosted off to Durham, Long Lartin in Worcestershire or somewhere like Leicester. The same, I knew, could happen to me. I suppose I was settling in as much as I could settle in to do my bird. I had enjoyed my chat with Reggie, but something wasn't right …

'Are you okay, Reggie?' I asked as I was about to step onto the landing. 'You don't look right. What's wrong?'

'I've been thinking about Frances a lot lately. Can't seem to get her out of my mind. These things come and go. It was the anniversary of her death the other day. It set me off.'

I went back in: 'Fancy some more tea?"

Reggie stood up, glanced along the landing and the young boys came trotting up. As I sat down another pot of tea appeared with fresh cups, sugar, milk and everything. I said nothing, waited until the tea brewed, and Reggie poured it out into two cups.

'It was the seventh of June – a sad, sad day for me. My wife died on that day, fourteen years ago, just under a year before we were arrested. I tried to give her everything. She had mental problems, you know that.'

'Really sorry, Reg,' I sympathised, putting my arm round his shoulders.

We sat there in silence for a few minutes. Reggie had his head in his hands. This powerful figure had only ever really had two women in his life: his mother, Violet, and Frances Shea. Frances was only twenty-three when she died in 1967, and the thought of it all haunted Reggie. I decided to say no more.

Well, I knew the whole story. In reality Frances had entered a world that she couldn't live in. Reggie bought her everything, but he owned her.

He expected her to do whatever he wanted. Frances was trapped in an environment that she knew nothing about. All around her, people were getting hurt. She wasn't used to that lifestyle and couldn't get out of it. Violet Kray was very protective of the twins, so if Frances had the hump about something she couldn't go to her mother-in-law.

Reggie, in his own way, couldn't see that he was doing anything wrong. Frances received everything she could wish for, apart from real love. She wasn't allowed to have a mind of her own; she was controlled from the moment she met Reggie. The entire romance had been a disaster. I felt for Reggie, whatever the rights or wrongs about how he had treated his wife.

Reggie collected his thoughts, sort of shook himself up and down, and regained his composure. He was trying to get Frances out of his mind.

As we shook hands, Reggie told me: 'When me and Ron get out we'll have a big house with a swimming pool. We'll have lots of land and we'll feel the wind in our faces. Some firms will get together and we'll have a mafia-type of operation going on. What do you think?'

'Good idea,' I smiled.

Perhaps Reggie had a premonition of the trouble that lay ahead. A few mornings later, after breakfast, he appeared in my cell. I was bending over, keeping my rusty pair of garden shears out of sight. Until then, only Neville the Devil had seen them.

Reggie went: 'What you got there?'

I had a quick check along the landing before producing my prized asset and making sure Reggie had a good look.

'I'm taking the nut off to make two blades. Look at those for weapons. Somebody smuggled them in, maybe from the garden. One of the crazy oddballs offered them to me. He was thinking I would want to cut through wire with them. I said I wasn't interested in that bollocks because I could see they would make a great weapon.'

'Just what I need,' Reggie nodded. 'How much do you want?'

'Hold up, you can have one of the blades for a tenner.'

'Done,' a pleased-looking Reggie grinned, slipping the newly acquired weapon under his shirt.

He got a good deal, and so did I. Without realising, Reggie paid for my blade, too, because I'd given a tenner to the oddball. Reggie hid his in one of the toilets by having a panel taken out. He wasn't too smart at that sort of thing. He had one of his little flunkies sorting that out for him. If the blade was found they would get nicked, and not him.

I couldn't stop thinking about the amount of bird that Reggie and Ronnie would have to serve. I couldn't imagine being sentenced to thirty years. They both had two decades left to survive. They wouldn't be getting out until the year 2000, if at all. So they would be approaching seventy years old.

There was no hope for Reggie and Ronnie. None at all.

CHAPTER EIGHT

THE BOMBERS
OF PARKHURST

'Why the fuck did you blow up the Old Bailey with our people inside? Our families were in there. They could have been killed.'

When I first arrived at Parkhurst, I'd found the antics of the IRA quite amusing. Hold up a minute, I thought, what are they doing? I looked into their cells when they were, standing to attention and all that. They had their ranks, although at first I thought it was a load of bollocks. They seemed to be playing soldiers and the other prisoners had a good laugh. As time passed, I began to respect them more and more. My attitude changed completely.

By 1981, I had learned more about them, and I also heard that Billy Armstrong, one of the IRA commanders responsible for the Old Bailey bombing, was due to be banged up with me.

There he was, reading a newspaper in one of the TV rooms. I looked the commander straight in the eye. Billy, a man who had devoted his life to a cause, stood his ground and stared straight back.

I'd always wanted to find out more about that attack in 1973. I knew the basic details. A car bomb blew up outside the Old Bailey and another went off near Scotland Yard. One bystander died – a sixty-year-old called Frederick Milton had a heart attack – and nearly 200 people were injured.

The bombings happened while I was at the peak of my powers with my shotgun, Kennedy, and carrying out lucrative armed robberies. Now, nearly a decade later, I had the chance to find out why Billy had put our friends and families at risk in the Old Bailey. I mean, there were cases going on all the time involving our boys.

Eleven of the IRA were involved, including the shortish, ordinary-looking Irishman standing in front of me. He looked like an everyday geezer you would see in the street, with his beard and glasses. The IRA prisoners came and went, between Albany, Parkhurst and other high security prisons. Now I had pinned Billy down, I hoped he could answer my questions. It turned out that he was more than happy to give me a bit of a lecture on the Troubles.

'The Old Bailey was a symbol of British domination,' he told me. 'In wars, there are always casualties. When someone comes out of a trench you don't know if it's a nice guy pointing a gun at you. You have to shoot him. War is war.'

'All right then,' I responded, changing tack to probe further. 'I can't work it out. We go at it to get money for our families and all that. I can't see me going out and planting a bomb, with the risk of getting killed, and not getting any money out of it.'

'The prize we are going for is much bigger than cash. You know, we've been going since just after the First World War. Ireland has been destroyed by the British and all we are doing is continuing the struggle, following in Michael Collins's footsteps, to get a united country. Northern Ireland must be freed from British rule.'

'Tell me more about Michael Collins,' I suggested. It was a fair question because, with all of my armed robberies and other criminal activities, I hadn't really thought too much about the events in Ireland. Now, with the new arrival joining a dedicated band of followers, I was keen to find out more about the Irish Republican Army.

'Michael Collins led the IRA in the War of Independence against Britain from 1919 until 1921. Did you know that your soldiers opened fire after a Gaelic football game and killed twelve people?'

'I didn't know that,' I admitted, thinking he was starting to make a speech. 'But that was a long time ago?'

Billy spat: 'The massacre may have been a long time ago, but nothing has changed. The year before the Old Bailey bomb, your soldiers opened fire at a civil rights march in Derry and killed another thirteen innocent people. That's why it's called Bloody Sunday.'

'No hope of a truce then,' I said, probably stating the obvious.

'No way. And you might have heard my father died recently?'

'Yes, I did hear. Some of the boys were talking on the wing. Sorry that your father passed away, with you so far from home.'

'I asked to go to the funeral in Ireland and they wouldn't let me. The IRA guys in here clubbed together to send some flowers, but that wasn't allowed. In the end a couple of Scots lads sent flowers. There's always been a strong connection between the Scots and the Irish, so I thought it was a great gesture by them.

'A lot of our people settled in Scotland after the Great Potato Famine in 1845. Two-thirds of the crop was lost because of disease. Even the big football teams now like Celtic and Hibs have Irish roots. We concentrate our attacks in England.'

Billy told me that, with the greatest of respect, we armed robbers were criminals. He and his supporters were political prisoners, fighting for a united Ireland. The one thing we all had in common, Billy said, was to disrupt the prison system and cause as much chaos as possible. The armed robbers wanted better conditions, more humane treatment of prisoners and a review of the parole system; the IRA had much more on their political agenda.

'Oh, and if you want to know how to make a bomb, we can show you how. We have experts in here who can show anyone how to make loads of weapons.'

'I'll bear that in mind,' I answered, thinking ahead that bombs instead of shotguns might not work for any future armed robberies.

All of the IRA men were known as Double Category 'A' – a step up from our level of notoriety. That meant much more attention from screws who noted every movement, gathering or anything unusual at all. I peeked inside Billy's cell. The IRA group had nothing apart from basic cell equipment. I was shocked that their superiors back in Ireland, with all of that funding, didn't do more for these men. The hierarchy certainly didn't look after their own people as far as I could see. With all those battalions operating, I thought the men in Parkhurst deserved more luxuries.

My fellow inmates weren't thugs off the street, who'd just been given a bomb to blow up. They'd been trained in places such as Libya, so they knew all the sophisticated ways of bomb-making and planning attacks. They still boiled over with anger over the policy of internment in 1971 when hundreds of Catholics were arrested. Internment was introduced under special powers, meaning that those suspected of having links with the IRA were imprisoned without trial. It happened after an intensified campaign against the security forces, with

British soldiers killed and kidnapped. Internment was generally seen as a failure because it caused unrest among the civilian population, who became willing to conceal suspects. The IRA gained many new recruits, too.

Father Pat Fell was one of theirs, doing a twelve-year stretch. I bumped into Fell on the Isle of Wight in 1981. He was nicked around 1973 for planning an IRA campaign in Coventry. He was actually an assistant priest there!

Catholics believe that a thin wafer of bread becomes the body of Jesus during the Communion ceremony. Fell was more likely to have something else in his mouth. He was a raving poof, and the IRA put him on charges for disgracing them.

The good Father never admitted to being an IRA volunteer. He was convicted of being a commander in an active service unit, but pleaded not guilty to everything. Mind you, we all denied charges against us. Cases had to be proved.

Fell did have a feather in his cap. Amazingly he won his case against the British government, accusing them of violating the European Convention on Human Rights. He had maintained that prisoners facing internal disciplinary charges should have the right to legal representation. I'll give him some respect for that one.

The Republican prisoners, with Fell as one of the leaders, held a sit-down protest over the way one of their group was treated. Both sides were injured when the screws tried to break up the protest. Fell appeared before the Board of Visitors who condemned him to nine days in solitary and more than five hundred days' loss of remission.

All the IRA men talked about Bobby Sands, the hunger striker who died for the cause while I was at Parkhurst. He was held in Maze prison in County Down, where he starved himself in protest against political status being taken away from IRA prisoners during the Troubles. He was even elected to the British Parliament while he was a prisoner. The death of Sands and several other supporters in 1981 led to a surge of IRA activity and trouble in other prisons.

At Parkhurst, a group of IRA men staged a three-day fast. I hadn't been involved with them on a day-to-day basis, apart from seeing them walking about on the landing or queuing at the hotplate in the days before their fast. The news from Ireland stirred up a lot of bad feeling – even among the regular prisoners because we were also behind bars.

'We would be happy to do the same as Bobby Sands if it came to it,' the IRA men told me.

We thought that, when men were willing to starve themselves to death, it was a different ball game. They were willing to die a horrible death for their beliefs.

The IRA protests really hit home with the prisoners at Parkhurst and Albany. These weren't just guys playing soldiers. They weren't there for the money or the glory. They were committed to the cause for one Ireland.

You have to be exceptionally brave to die from hunger. We weren't worried about whether hunger strikers involved the IRA or another terrorist group; if someone starved himself to death, it was serious business. There wasn't much we could do apart from asking after the welfare of our hunger strikers and offering bits and pieces, like tobacco, to those who were looking after and supporting them.

The IRA group at Parkhurst were taken down to the punishment block after they started their fast. This was because they could have stirred things up, and involved everyone in political talk. They returned, alive and incredibly hungry, after their protest, although many more riots and demonstrations lay ahead at prisons throughout the country. I knew that if our IRA people had deteriorated, they would have been taken to the hospital wing.

I met Ronnie McCartney late in 1981. He was a small guy with dark hair and a stocky build. He was convicted of trying to kill three policemen in the 1970s.

'How would you feel if Bradford became a colony of India?' Ronnie asked me. 'You would be in uproar, wanting to fight for your country. That's exactly what has happened in Ireland.'

I don't believe in people blowing up pubs or anything like that. If there's a war, I believe in soldiers fighting soldiers. All of this commitment to a cause made me think, though.

Ronnie said he was willing to go on hunger strike that same year. He lodged a will, granting power of attorney to a friend who was trusted to let him die if he lapsed into a coma. That eased the pressure on Ronnie's family. The IRA, though, decided that it would be too difficult to manage hunger strikes in too many places.

Some IRA protests took a different form.

'What's that pong?' I asked a group of screws one morning as my cell door was opened. 'It seems to have just wafted in along the wing. Has everyone shit themselves?'

I had done my business in my pot and was preparing to go to the slops sink and empty it out. This smell, however, was so strong that I could hardly notice the aroma from the pathetic contents of my pot.

'It's a dirty protest,' a tubby screw answered as his belly wobbled up and down. 'Somebody from the IRA has covered himself in shit. They want better treatment, but I can't see that helping their cause.'

Shortly afterwards a couple of IRA men told me that, in the event of a nuclear attack or during a civil war, all men were to be shot their cells. They said they'd raided the governor's office in another nick and took a secret document, showing how the Army would carry out the killings.

The IRA tried to smuggle a gun into Parkhurst around that time. A barrel was discovered in a training shoe, with other parts found in clothing. If the plot had succeeded, they would have shot the screws.

The IRA prisoners spent all of their time plotting. It was total commitment to make Ireland one country, away from

Great Britain. They hated the British government, the screws and the Ulster Volunteer Force, who were fighting to keep Northern Ireland under British rule. These opposing groups were kept well apart in the prison system.

The IRA prisoners had their own set of rules and disciplinary procedures. If one of them did something that wasn't right, there would be a court martial and a range of punishments. All of this was happening in the cells on 'B' wing!

At Parkhurst I met a new arrival, Paddy Joe Hill, early in 1982. Paddy was one of the 'Birmingham Six' who were ghosted around the prison system. I spotted him on his own on the landing, looking over the railings. I didn't know who he was at the time, but we quickly became acquainted. I could see that he needed someone to talk to.

This was not a tall, muscular or intimidating man. He must have been shorter than me, about five-foot-five, slim, with dark hair and a face full of passion and anger. I gave my usual introduction and prepared to find out more.

Twenty-one people died, and nearly two hundred were injured, when two Birmingham pubs were bombed on 21 November 1974. They were the Mulberry Bush and Tavern in the Town. A third bomb, in the doorway of a Barclays bank, failed to detonate.

There was a delay in issuing the warning because phone boxes were vandalised. Apparently the caller, using the correct IRA code, phoned local newspapers but didn't state the exact location of the bombs. One of the pubs was at the base of the massive Rotunda building and the other was a few yards away. Other buildings near the Rotunda were damaged and people were injured by flying glass.

Along with Hugh Callaghan, Gerard Hunter, Richard McIlkenny, Billy Power and John Walker, Paddy was jailed for life in 1975. There was terror on the mainland in the seventies because of the IRA bombing campaign, and the Old Bill was desperate to nick the Birmingham bombers. They were keen to nick anyone who appeared to be a good fit.

'The police knew we didn't do it. They even told us they believed we were not guilty,' Paddy almost shouted, his voice full of venom. 'They didn't care that we were innocent. They set out to frame us.'

Paddy said he was never a member of the IRA. He collected money for people who were interned, and that was all.

'The police kicked and punched me. They said they would kick me to death if I didn't make a statement. Even if I got off, they said they would tell the IRA I had been squealing and so I would be shot. They tried to make me sign a statement. Gerry Hunter and I refused to sign. The others were false confessions. You can see that. They've got the facts wrong about where the bombs were planted and everything. Justice? What a joke.'

Paddy told me he had been in trouble with the police before. He'd been banged up for stabbing and slicing people. Now he was trapped in the 'merry-go-round' of the prison system, being sent from high security jail to high security jail, spending much of his time in solitary. He said the screws pissed and spat in his food, and even laced it with shards of glass, in various prisons during his high security confinement in the seventies.

'I was guilty of my violent past. I accepted that. But a blind man would be able to tell that the six of us were totally innocent of the bombings. It's one of the worst miscarriages of justice ever. We were fitted up because it was easy. I'll fight on for justice until my dying day.'

I could tell, then, that Paddy Hill had been wrongly convicted. Hearing his story made me seethe with anger.

'I have to give credit to your Dr Cooper,' Paddy said, continuing his story and referring to the head psychiatrist at Parkhurst. 'I've just been to see him.'

'Oh, what happened?'

'Well, he could have had me nutted off. He had so many reasons to have me sectioned. He said he knew I was innocent and what I was going through.'

Hearing that was just incredible – even Dr Cooper could tell what was going on.

As for the IRA members at Parkhurst, I noticed that, as their sentences wore on, they adapted to life in jail like the rest of us. Some of them had been in much longer than me – about ten years in some cases. They bought and sold puff and many of them got stoned out of their heads.

Love them or hate them, the IRA made their mark on Parkhurst and Albany. To me, they appeared as ordinary people who lived their lives the same as everyone else.

The difference was, they hated Britain with a passion – and were prepared to kill for their cause.

CHAPTER NINE
COPS AND CLOCKS

Fat Fred Sewell, the jewellery box maker, killed a top copper as far back as 1971. He went the whole way, shooting the highest-ranking officer ever to die on the streets of Britain. That meant Fat Fred was destined for a long, long stretch behind bars: thirty years.

I usually caught up with Fat Fred on the twos, just ambling around and minding his own business. I never saw him doing much socialising, as he seemed to be in a world of his own. I would describe Fred as portly, with a chubby face and a fat little body. He had black hair with a parting and sideburns going down to the bottom of his ears. That was always his style.

Now, I have to tell you that Fred was involved in a disastrous raid on a jewellery shop in Blackpool.

Fred and another four determined robbers drove from London in two stolen cars: a green Triumph 2000 and a bronze Ford Capri. They had a sawn-off shotgun, an automatic pistol and two revolvers.

They burst into Preston's Jewellers at just after 9.30am on Monday, 23 August 1971. Fat Fred was carrying the shotgun. The Triumph waited nearby while the Capri was parked out of sight.

Everything that could go wrong did go wrong.

The manager was in a repair room, unknown to Fat Fred and his mates. He heard what was going on and activated a silent alarm. A fireman came into the shop, also saw what was happening and told another shop-keeper to call the police. One of the gang knocked the fireman spark out.

Fat Fred told me how they made off with trays of jewellery. Fred tried to get into the Triumph, but a panda car blocked the road and then crashed into Fred's motor.

Thing went from bad to worse as Fred and his colleagues piled into the Triumph and reversed out of the street in an effort to reach the Capri. The same copper blocked their path again, but Fred, at the wheel, shunted it out of the way. Another determined officer appeared in a panda car and followed them. One of the gang got out of the Triumph and shot him in the arm. The bullet went through his chest, narrowly missing his heart. Somehow, despite his injuries, the wounded copper managed to radio for help.

After more heavy cops-and-robbers escapades, with more shots being fired, Superintendent Gerald Richardson – the head of Blackpool Police – joined the fray.

Now on foot, Fat Fred lumbered towards a van being driven along a street. The van stopped and Richardson caught up with Fat Fred. The top copper told him to give up his pistol, but that was never going to happen.

'Richardson, well I didn't know then he was the head of Blackpool Police, tackled me around the neck and we fell onto the side of the van.'

Fred's gun went off. One bullet pierced the top copper's sleeve and the other went into his stomach. Fred ordered the people in the van to get out and he drove off. The superintendent died in hospital.

The gang were all tracked down and arrested; it took six weeks to find Fred, who was convicted of murder.

Gerald Richardson was awarded the George Cross posthumously and another copper, Carl Walker, also received the George Cross; an assortment of other awards went to the other policemen.

Hold up a minute, when I first met this guy standing in front of me on the landing at Parkhurst, he looked harmless enough. And yet he'd killed a top copper, attracting all the hate of the Old Bill and the country. The streets of Blackpool were lined by 100,000 people for the superintendent's funeral. He was dressed in full uniform in his coffin. The service was at St John's church where he'd been married a few years beforehand. There were 400 coppers lining the route and another 300 following the hearse.

'Be careful what you say to Fat Fred,' a couple of the boys told me. 'He might feed it back to security to help with his parole.'

I decided to make up my own mind. There were always character assassinations in prison, and if people didn't like a guy they would say he was 'iffy'.

'Fancy a cup of tea?' Fred asked.

'On my way,' I replied.

Fred took me down to his cell on the ones and poured me a cup of tea. He also produced a couple of cheese sandwiches, so I tucked in.

'I was going to shoot him in the foot or leg. Next thing the gun went off even though I hardly touched the trigger. I said that at the trial but they weren't having it. Now, every day, I see the copper coming towards me. He was far too brave. Far too brave.'

'Yeah, he shouldn't have died,' I agreed, thinking about the hair trigger.

'I got a helluva beating off the Old Bill. But that happens if they lose one of their own. They'd just done away with capital punishment and I could easily have been hanged.'

I could see that Fred often reflected on his crime because his face was etched with emotion.

'I've taken away someone's husband and someone's father. That's what I find hard to handle.'

Many years later, I heard that Fred had written to the superintendent's wife, apologising for his crime.

Most of the chaps in Parkhurst and Albany could justify what they'd done. If they'd robbed a bank, they could say the bankers were stealing money from people anyway. If they shot a gangster, they could say he was a villain and members of the public weren't hurt. It was different for Fred because he hadn't meant to kill the brave copper.

I know you'll be thinking that Fat Fred shouldn't have had a gun in the first place. I would say that there are kids out on the street nowadays with guns. Weapons shouldn't be available. As well as the guy using them, it's the geezer who is supplying them that we need to cut out.

If you're living in that world, in the gangster world, everyone is carrying a gun and you've got to carry a weapon to protect yourself. You're not going out to shoot people; you're going out to look after yourself. If a villain pulls a gun on you, he isn't doing it for a fucking laugh.

He's going to shoot you, so it's best that you whack him first.

Fat Fred had a colourful background. I knew he ran car lots, on the outside. I believe he got involved in the bit of work because he didn't have too much dough at the time and wanted to get some better cars for his business.

I spotted a property magazine in his cell during our chat and pointed out to Fred that sites like his in south London had rocketed in value.

'How much did you pay for one of your places in that area?'

'Oh, at least a couple of grand,' Fred remembered.

'Well, that was a long time ago,' I pointed out. 'Look at this. I reckon your site there is worth a couple of million quid.'

Fat Fred's eyes nearly popped out of his head. He hadn't realised that he was really a multi-millionaire with the dramatic rise in property prices! Perhaps he hadn't needed to go on the Blackpool job after all.

'Bobby, can I ask you something? I've only ever been in here. What are the other prisons like? Have you had anything worse than here?'

I decided to tell Fred about my most horrific experience. In a way, it channelled so much of my energy against the system. I resented the buildings, the screws, the food ... you name it, I built up pure hatred. If I detested the prison system before my appalling experience, that disgust was increased tenfold. They tried to remove my independence and suck away any signs of personality. My energy levels, opposing the authorities, were monumental.

'I had a bad time when I was doing bird for manslaughter. I was at the Aylesbury Young Offenders place. They said I was the most violent person there, and one day a doctor came up to me and said I was to receive some special attention.

'He got a couple of screws to take me to a medical room. I remember everything was white and the doctor had on a white coat. He gave me some pills to take. I thought, "What's going on here?" I assumed they were sedatives or something to stop me being so violent. Well, the room went round and round, and then I was taken to a van and driven off somewhere.

'I arrived at another prison, God knows where, and I remember screws saying to keep the cuffs on me because I was so violent. I ended up in the whitest white room I can imagine and a doctor, again all in white, gave me some more tablets. Maybe he didn't know I had been given the previous lot. Whatever the truth, I was totally and completely stoned.'

'Sounds like they were carrying out some sort of experiment,' a puzzled Fred said.

'It got worse. They put me on a chair and took my shirt off, leaving me in my trousers. I remember a geezer appeared, holding a set of electrodes with suckers on the end. All of the suckers were attached to my head and body. Not only that, they'd injected some sort of jelly into the suckers.'

'This is incredible,' Fred shouted, startled.

'After that, some sort of strobe light kept flashing in my face, making lots of bangs. I felt a current passing through me, causing me to jolt backwards and forwards. I'm sure it happened just a few times, but for me it went on forever, and sweat was pouring off me in little rivers. Everything was a blur, but I did see a couple of guys writing down whatever they had achieved. I suppose it was some sort of record of my reaction. I must have passed out.

'I woke up, back in my cell in Aylesbury. I'll never forget the look on the face of a bloke called Ward, one of the screws. He shook his head and seemed upset. I was covered in red marks from the suckers. The whole episode had taken him totally by surprise, too.

'I was ghosted off to other prisons while the wounds healed so, by the time visitors were allowed to see me, I was almost back to my normal self. My sister Pauline tried hard to get to the bottom of all this, but she was met with a stone wall. No one knew of any paperwork to explain what had gone on.'

Fred was still gobsmacked. 'Bizarre. Totally bizarre. I've never heard anything like that in my life.'

'Me neither. It's haunted me ever since. So that's the answer to your question a while back.'

Most of Fred's spare hours were spent lovingly making clocks. Yes, clocks. His cell was packed with pieces of wood, matchsticks, clock parts and all that. Fred's skill was amazing. He made cuckoo clocks, some with a fairy going round and others that played 'Edelweiss' from *The Sound of Music*. How did he do that? I've no idea.

'How weird is Fred?' Reggie commented more than once. 'He's doing life with a thirty-year rec. I doubt if he'll get out after shooting a copper. So he's sitting there watching the time tick by, doing time, and making clocks! He's got to be off his rocker.'

Fat Fred's jewellery boxes, valuable currency in Parkhurst, were the real deal. He even lined them with blue or red felt. Fat Fred was under suspicion when a section of green felt disappeared from a pool table. When the screws had a good look they could see he didn't use green for his boxes! So Fat Fred was in the clear.

After a decade in the nick, Fat Fred fell in love. I used to go to English classes with him. However, Fat Fred wasn't improving his education; he fell for an old girl who came from the mainland to teach English. She really was an old girl and all, with a few wrinkles to show she had lived a bit. I learned about where to put full stops and commas, and nicked a few pens and pencils as well.

'That's a smart bird,' Fred whispered as we sat there, beside a couple of London armed robbers, listening to the old girl going on about Shakespeare and his plays.

'She is an old bird,' I pointed out, looking at her gnarled face and stooped shoulders.

'Quite tasty,' Fred answered, baffling me with his choice of woman. 'Shame I can't take it any further. Look at the body.'

I looked at the body, although she didn't do anything for me. The shape was still there, just, and I suppose she tried to look sexy with painted nails and high heels. Basically, she was well past her best.

I have no idea whether the old girl shared the same feelings. The circumstances knocked any notion of romance on the head. There was no chance of any groping.

Fred, anxious for some action with the old girl, had no choice but to use up his energy making more of those bloody clocks.

CHAPTER TEN

A NEW ARRIVAL: THE YORKSHIRE RIPPER

I was used to seeing high security convoys coming and going, transporting the country's most dangerous men. As I endured 1981 inside Britain's Alcatraz, my attention was drawn to a collection of vans rumbling through the gates of Parkhurst. Who could this be?

No one could make out the prisoner through the largest truck's darkened windows. The latest inmate had a full head of frizzy, nearly black hair, a funny-shaped beard and moustache and dark staring eyes. We were horrified to find out that the new guest of Her Majesty was the Yorkshire Ripper.

There was no way he could have survived a day on our wing. Sex offenders, rapists, nonces and those types would have been torn apart. That was why he was taken to the Vulnerable Prisoners Unit – for his own safety apart from anything else.

The Ripper went on a killing spree across Greater Manchester and Yorkshire between 1975 and 1980. He targeted prostitutes because he believed he was on a mission from God.

The Old Bill never even had Sutcliffe down as a suspect. He was interviewed several times at home and, as his wife supported his insistence he had been in the house at the crucial times, she therefore ended up giving him alibis. They never found anything in his car or garage. The Old Bill said he had been clever to hide everything and lucky to escape attention while he killed.

Fair play to the judge, Mr Justice Boreham. Sutcliffe's defence and the Attorney General had accepted the view of doctors that Sutcliffe was a paranoid schizophrenic and should be hospitalised instead of jailed. Sutcliffe insisted that he was acting on instructions from God because he heard messages coming from a graveyard at Bingley in West Yorkshire.

What a load of bollocks. The judge demanded that the trial should go ahead, the jury found him sane and guilty of thirteen murders plus seven attempted murders. Mr Justice Boreham said he was handing down twenty life sentences, with a recommendation of at least thirty years – an unusually long period for 'an unusually dangerous man'. He said they were murders of a very cowardly quality.

'It is difficult to find words that are adequate in my judgement to describe the brutality and the gravity of these offences, and I say at once I am not going to pause to seek those words. I am prepared to let the catalogue of your crimes speak for itself.'

There was a lot of discontentment that the Ripper had turned up in Parkhurst. The general feeling was that they should have brought back hanging, just for him.

The usual dark humour was there from the start. I remember one of the kitchen prisoners, playing a prank, and running through to tell us that the Ripper was going to work in there making sweets and desserts.

'I'm not having that,' I said. 'We'll have a sit-down or whatever it takes to stop this. How could he get a job in the kitchen? We'll whack him!'

'He's going to be cutting up all the tarts.'

A lot of the Ripper's paintings started coming onto the main wing. Actually, he had a bit of talent. The paintings were quite good, really. People started buying them up to see if they could make any money out of them when they were released. The paintings usually had a religious theme, with Christ on the cross or with his disciples. You have to remember that the Ripper went all religious in jail – even more so than during his frenzy of murders.

One Sunday, just a few weeks after the Ripper arrived, I decided to go to church. There was little else to do apart from read or do exercises, so I thought I would have a flick through the Bible and join in the hymns. I was never into prayers and all that game, but it did pass the time. The scene that enfolded in front of me took some believing.

When I arrived I could see the service already taking place, with the vicar wearing his robes and dog collar, telling a story about Jesus. When that finished an organ played and I watched as a geezer marched up the aisle carrying a pole with a golden cross on the top. He wore what looked like a choirboy's outfit, covered with a red gown and a gold 'V' on the front.

The face looked familiar. Dark hair, a beard ... bloody hell, it was the Yorkshire Ripper!

'It's him, isn't it?' I heard whispers around me.

'He must feel nearer to God with the high pole,' I heard someone behind me giggle.

The Ripper was safe enough in the church, but not so secure in the hospital wing. Sutcliffe was attacked by a Scottish prisoner called Jimmy Costello in January 1983. At the time, the Ripper was in F2 wing of the hospital where his mental state was being assessed.

Jimmy wasn't the ideal person for the Ripper to bump into. For a start, he'd been in court nearly thirty times and had received fifteen prison sentences. A lot of it involved firearms. Unfortunately for Sutcliffe, Jimmy had been diagnosed as mentally ill and was awaiting transfer to Broadmoor. In his fragile mental state, he was like a ticking time bomb, ready to explode in the Ripper's face.

One day, the Ripper's cell was unlocked and he went into a recess to fill a plastic bowl with hot water, maybe to wash or something like that. He turned off the tap and then headed back to his cell. He said Jimmy appeared with a broken coffee jar and lashed out.

Jimmy's version of events was that Sutcliffe attacked him after a row over a newspaper story. Jimmy said the Ripper had used his artist's paint to blot out an article about vice and prostitutes, and that wasn't the first time. Jimmy's case was that he was acting in self-defence.

The Ripper copped a deep cut running from his mouth to his neck and another one from his left eye to his ear. Altogether he needed thirty stitches. At the time I thought it was a shame that Jimmy didn't cause more damage. Nowadays, of course, I try to find non-violent solutions, although I do have hatred for people like Sutcliffe.

Jimmy was found guilty of wounding Peter Sutcliffe with intent to cause him grievous bodily harm. He received five years on top of his sentence. He swore at the jurors and, as he was driven away from court, yelled: 'How can anyone use too much violence against the Ripper?'

Frankie Fraser appeared on the wing again, shortly after the attack on the Ripper. I told him all about the unwelcome newcomer, how we were kept away from him and the attack with the broken coffee jar.

Frankie's verdict? 'Jimmy Costello deserves a medal.'

CHAPTER ELEVEN

CHARLIE RICHARDSON AND THE BLACK BOX

'I didn't do that torture stuff, understand? I gave them a few right handers, but I didn't use any black boxes.'

I could hear Charlie Richardson, just a few cells away, talking to the stocky, grey-haired, middle-aged screw who was unlocking the cells in the morning. It was eight o'clock. Charlie had disappeared into the dispersal system somewhere, but he was back and making his point.

I was intrigued by the conversation, and could hardly believe that I was on the same landing with some of the most infamous gangsters of all time. I was keen to meet Charlie properly, but thought I should let him finish his debate with the warder.

'They jailed you for torture,' the screw said, slowly and deliberately, as I remained rooted to the spot, taking in every word.

'Let me tell you this, right? I had an office in Park Lane, understand? I was running my scrapyards and everything. Yeah, I had a few bent coppers in tow and I was a naughty boy, with all the rackets going on. You know what they claimed I did?'

The screw had heard Charlie protesting before. 'I think I know.'

'They said I staged mock trials. Well, that's what they said. They said I handed out beatings and Frankie Fraser pulled out teeth with pliers. If anyone crossed me, they did get a right hander or two and that was all. You know what else they were alleging?'

'I've a feeling you're going to tell me,' said the grumpy screw.

'They said I nailed someone to the floor. A nail in his foot, they said.'

'I know the story,' the screw grumbled, checking inside Charlie's cell.

'You know what else they said? They claimed I made someone mop up his blood with his underpants.'

'You haven't mentioned the black box.'

'Yeah, the black box,' Charlie raged. 'They brought a contraption into the court and said I used it as an implement of torture. It looked like some old-fashioned generator with a handle on it and a couple of leads.'

'I read all about it in the papers,' the screw cut in.

'Can you believe I attached the wires to men's nipples and genitals to give an electric shock? I even read that I did it while my victim was in a bath to increase the pain. What a load of rubbish. That's why I keep applying for parole. Understand?'

'Well, they gave you twenty-five years, so I would say you've at least another ten years to go. You're nearly fifty now – you'll be an old man when you get out!'

'Bah,' Charlie grunted.

'Good luck with the parole!'

It was a regular topic of conversation in Parkhurst. There were stories about Charlie staging those mock trials in his scrapyard, with the main man himself as the judge and brother Eddie as the prosecution. Other members of the firm took on the role of the defence, allegedly, but they never won any cases! The story went that they had wigs and gowns stolen from the Old Bailey to add a touch of realism. The punishment for anyone found guilty, of course, was the dreaded black box ... allegedly.

Charlie had grown up around the bomb craters of Camberwell in south London. He scavenged on bomb sites with his young mates during the war years. I did the same thing, of course, during the fifties, when new developments were springing up but craters were still plentiful.

There was rationing and a desperate need for everyday essentials. Frankie Fraser, later to become Charlie's enforcer, was nicking stuff all over the place around the same time. Frankie never forgave the Nazis for surrendering. The shortages meant that people would be flocking to see him, just for everyday goods.

Charlie stole lead from roofs, nicked motors, bought and sold stuff and developed a shrewd business brain while still a young boy. His speciality was breaking into a lorry, unloading whatever was on it and selling everything on for good money.

Barely out of his teens, he owned six scrapyards in south London with a turnover of £250,000 a year. He paid the Old Bill to stay away and not find out if he was buying stolen gear. Eventually, Charlie said, he was paying off commanders at Scotland Yard to keep their noses out of his affairs.

Charlie maintained he'd been given such a hefty prison sentence because he was a pawn in a big political game. He bugged Harold Wilson's office for the South Africans, who thought the prime minister was a communist with sympathies for the African National Congress, or ANC. Charlie found out who cleaned Wilson's office, arranged for the bugging, and then drove to the airport to send the tape to South Africa.

Charlie was 'king of the long-firm fraud'. That meant a company was set up, with goods paid for on time. An excellent credit rating was built up. A huge order would be placed, without payment – then Charlie's operation and the goods would vanish. Radios, fancy goods, crockery and household essentials would turn up in markets and second-hand shops.

Charlie escaped from a lower security prison in 1980 and spent nearly a year 'on the trot' in Europe.

There was a surprise in store for me after the heated debate about the black box. Gary Wilson, an armed robber and one of the closest people to the man himself, popped his head into my cell: 'Charlie wants to speak to you.'

I quickly gathered my thoughts and followed Gary along the corridor. I followed him into Charlie's cell, which was dominated by a large table and piles of books and newspapers. Charlie was well groomed, as I always preferred to be. His grey hair was receding at the front, and he was growing a goatee beard. He was wearing an ironed shirt, although I could see a T-shirt and shorts folded beside his bed, ready for a change later.

Charlie's steely blue eyes almost pierced into me, like some sort of silent interrogation. I didn't feel threatened; I just felt that he was totally in control and genuinely interested in me.

'You're running the money lending in here.'

I admitted my current role, hardly expecting him to require a tenner. Gary poured tea for the three of us, and I was surprised to hear what Charlie had to say next. He pointed out that I was too smart to be a thug. I should abandon life with a gun. I should be thinking about going straight.

'We're all learning lessons in here. The future is education. You can make a lot of money in straight business. That's what I'm planning now. And you can do the same.'

We shook hands, firmly, and Gary poured out more tea. I knew that I had met someone with a special part to play in my life.

In the sixties, Charlie operated his manor in south London with brother Eddie, while the Krays ruled east London. In the seventies, my manor in north London stretched from Highbury Corner to Archway, to Finsbury Park and Caledonian Road. There was no overlap of areas.

I was surprised that two notorious, respected leaders of men were on reasonable terms. Now I was sat at his table, I asked Charlie why he and Reggie got on okay despite the murder of George Cornell, various gangland feuds and general animosity between the firms.

'You just have to get on with it in here,' Charlie responded. 'We're on the same landing, understand? He's not a bad bloke. The Krays don't have the skill or cunning of the Richardsons. They can be like bulls in china shops. I get on with Reggie all right. I have him in the cell for tea. Ronnie still hates my guts, though. I hear he writes to Reggie, saying how much he hates me.'

'I saw some of the letters a while ago. I don't know if you were mentioned or not, because it was just a scrawl!'

It was time for breakfast, so we went down the staircase to collect it from the hotplate on the ones. It was near what was known as the 'happy hatch' where people on medication could collect their medical supplies for the day ahead. There was always a queue there, with confused prisoners waiting on anything from plasters to their daily doses of prescribed drugs. No wonder so many of them looked off their heads, adding the concoction from the happy hatch to their puff of drugs or whatever.

A reluctant group of inmates manned the hotplate, serving out the early morning grub – lots of prisoners didn't like working on the hotplate because there was a danger of being stabbed if you short-changed someone with a small portion. Gary got involved talking to a couple of chaps in the queue. Charlie and I surveyed the options: cornflakes, porridge (what else?); eggs, bacon, tomatoes and beans with a choice of tea or coffee.

By now I was used to Parkhurst's uninspiring meals. At dinnertime (that was what we called lunchtime) you could have the meat of the day with potatoes, beans, peas and carrots. Sometimes chips were on offer, with fish on Fridays. There was also a menu for vegetarians. The middles were cut out of tomatoes and filled with veg. Special meals were prepared for Jews and Muslims.

Both Parkhurst and Wormwood Scrubs had a reputation for allowing you as much bread as you liked with all of your meals. In other nicks you might be restricted to one or two slices of bread or a roll or two at dinnertime and at teatime.

A lot of the grub was sent back to the kitchen. They used to buy the worst ingredients and produced some crap food. Sometimes the potatoes were black – I don't know how that happened – and the veg was often boiled to within an inch of its life.

On Sunday we had roast beef, and that might sound like a good meal, but it was one slice of beef cut so thin you could almost see through it. They would put the veg in to boil at maybe six o'clock in the morning, but it wouldn't be eaten until lunchtime, so all the goodness would be gone. It turned into a mush. Some people bought a jar of jam or Marmite from the canteen out of their wages, took some bread from the hotplate area, and survived on sandwiches.

There was an alternative to collecting food from the hotplate. You could cook your own grub on the wings. Four or five prisoners would put their wages together to get what we called a food boat. Say you were working as a cleaner and had money coming in, you could put in £3 a week or something like that. You could order a whole chicken for £1.50 or £2.50, depending on the size. So £20 would buy a few chickens. A member of staff would go to the local shops and buy the food that had been ordered by the prisoners. You could buy other ingredients from the canteen and become quite self-sufficient.

We had a freezer and a fridge on the wing. Each day you could collect veg from the hotplate and cook your own meat. There were a couple of cookers with ovens on the wing, as well as sinks and worktops to prepare the meals. Cooking food was a way of giving the prisoners some freedom.

For the breakfast with Charlie, I chose some basic-looking cornflakes, as well as eggs on toast. Charlie opted for a similar arrangement, plus sausages and bacon.

'You're settling in well to Britain's Alcatraz,' Charlie winked at me. 'Come back to my cell. I always eat there around that big table.'

I followed Charlie back up the stairs. Gary was in the cell already along with Hassan, Gaddafi's hitman in the UK. I had another look at Charlie's table. It had to be three times the size of the one in Reggie's cell.

Gary, a blond-haired and blue-eyed guy, was well respected in Parkhurst. He was the same age as me, about thirty, never said a bad word about anyone and was totally loyal. I didn't do any work with him because he operated in south London. He enjoyed listening to Charlie when he talked about minerals – diamonds and other precious gems – and how to run a business.

There was quite a difference between Gary and Hassan. Gary was about five-foot-nine, while Hassan was around nine inches taller with the blackest, curliest hair I'd ever seen.

I started to chat: 'I bet they wanted to lock me away on my own forever. I didn't expect to be able to mix with you boys after threatening the governor with a blade over at Albany. They said I took him hostage. I suppose I did, because I wouldn't let him go until I reached my cell. I feel I've been here for ages now – I suppose this place deserves to be called Britain's Alcatraz with the sea and all that.'

The well-read Charlie was well informed: 'I've read the book about the American version – it's called *Escape from Alcatraz*. It's a good read. You can get it through the library here.'

'The film might be worth watching,' I joined in, trying to display knowledge about the infamous island in San Francisco Bay.

'Even Clint Eastwood wouldn't be able to get out of Parkhurst,' Charlie grinned as he attacked a well-done scrawny sausage.

'I hear all the escape attempts end in failure, so I'm not going to bother,' I said.

'Yeah, they're always unsuccessful. They watch us in Category "A" night and day.'

'Not sure about the bacon today,' Gary chipped in. 'Nez must have been busy again.'

'Nez is back in his cell having a bit of Muriel,' Charlie joked.

The target of his humour was Nizamodeen Hosein. 'Nez' had intended to kidnap Rupert Murdoch's wife, but instead captured the wife of the tycoon's deputy chairman. Nez and his brother wanted £1 million in ransom money. The pile of cash wasn't forthcoming, so Muriel McKay was fed to the pigs on a farm in Hertfordshire. All of this meant that Nez was asked most mornings if he was enjoying the bacon, presumably as there was a bit of Muriel in the pork.

'I can't taste any Muriel in this slice,' Charlie continued to laugh, twirling the bacon around his fork.

It was a pretty grim joke about such a brutal crime, but making light of such horrors has always been the way in prison.

Some prisoners ate in the association areas, places where they could meet and have a chat, but after I had officially met Charlie, I seemed to always be eating in his cell. I felt more at home there. Another meal time, Charlie said to me, 'Bobby, I can see you have a brain, running the finances and working as the fixer. I've got a long time left in here, but you could be out in five or six years if you behave yourself. As I've said before, the best way is education.'

Charlie pointed to the pile of books on his table and others in the corners of his cell. Magazine pages were opened on articles about minerals, world affairs and stock prices.

'The Open University is the way forward, Bobby. I've studied for O-levels and A-levels, and I've been doing an Open University course to get a sociology degree. It'll help you go straight when you get out. I'll ask if you can go on a course. Want to give it a go? I've been doing all sorts of correspondence courses. Now they have a special education unit at Maidstone, dedicated to studying.'

I could only agree with what he was saying. Day after day, I saw him studying his books, gaining more and more knowledge. It struck me that if he was released, with his business skills added to extra qualifications and desire, he would be a formidable force in any trade.

'I can see what it's doing for you. I've been getting through a lot of reading and listening to debates on the radio. If you can put in a word, I'm up for it.'

Charlie's cell was such a friendly, welcoming place to be. The association areas had tables with chairs, and people played cards, but you didn't always feel safe mixing with people you hardly knew anything about.

One morning, Nez was the centre of attention in the queue at the hotplate. This time, there was no bacon involved.

Everything had appeared peaceful enough when the cells opened.

I headed for Charlie Richardson's cell, and we waited for a member of his firm to bring in hot water for our tea. After the water arrived, we had a quick chat and made our move down the staircase to the hotplate.

Everything kicked off in a flash as we stood in the queue. Further along the line a blade was produced. It glinted in the lights around the hotplate before plunging into the unsuspecting body of Francis McGee.

The attacker was John Paton, who had plenty of form. He'd been sentenced to life at Leeds Crown Court for murdering an inmate at Wakefield prison in 1976. The victim then was Robert Houston, twenty-three, who was attacked with a bed leg.

I'd heard about Paton and made deliberate attempts to stay well clear. Paton was an expert at brewing hooch, that home-made booze using potato peelings and fruit.

The version I heard was that Paton had accused Houston of stealing some of the hooch and launched into him with the leg from the bed.

'He's done it before, you know,' Nez shouted out as a ring of people tried to intervene in our breakfast queue. 'Grab Paton, someone.'

An arm from somewhere managed to restrain Paton, but it was too late. Paton's weapon, a piece of filed-down steel, had plunged into his victim nine or ten times. Screws appeared from everywhere, shouting and trying to reach McGee's bloodied body.

Who else but Nez had McGee's head in his lap: 'It was over a game of chess, you know. McGee here cheated, and Paton didn't forgive him. That's what it was all about. The guy went back to his cell and got the weapon. Looks like this bloke is dead.'

A bunch of screws took over, trying desperately to stop the blood spurting out of McGee. It was spraying everywhere. Nez was right. There was no hope. We were all led back to our cells and locked up again while the mess was sorted out. Anyone who had managed to get served took their breakfasts back with them.

The prisoners didn't want anything like that happening again. If you were a bit dodgy the inmates would suss you out. Everyone would be there, looking, when someone arrived on the landing with their box of possessions. A delegation would enter the new prisoner's cell and ask for background details. 'Who are you? What are you in for?'

If the delegation wasn't satisfied with the answers, the geezer under suspicion would have to contact his brief to provide papers and statements within seven days. If those didn't materialise, it was in the prisoner's interests to disappear down the punishment block or somehow arrange a transfer. Threats made against him could never be taken lightly.

Another afternoon, after counting my highly illegal banking profits, I headed along to Charlie's cell for a general chat. I thought he might be able to advise me on expanding my operation. But he had other plans of his own ...

'I've got a fantastic business idea for this place,' Charlie told me, full of enthusiasm, as soon as I arrived. 'It's easy to organise, gives the boys something to do and makes money at the same time. You can help me to fix all this. The cash can go to a charity or something like that.'

'Legally make money in here?' I answered, wondering how he could make a few quid in our surroundings without starting a scam. 'I'm making a few quid, but it ain't legit.'

Charlie pointed to a sheet of paper on his table. I looked closely, not knowing what to expect. There was nothing about loans, fixing or using Neville the Devil as enforcer! Charlie was definitely following a legal route with his scheme.

He had a business plan all drawn out. The sheet of paper contained diagrams, profit and loss tables, and lots of figures. I had no idea what it all meant.

'Recycling, boy,' Charlie grinned. 'Look at the mound of newspapers and all the other stuff that comes in here every day. Tons if it can be used again. They could do this in every prison. Good for the environment, too, re-using things instead of throwing it all away. All the paper can be compressed to make bricks for barbecues or even fire-places. Look at this.'

I could see his point. Even in Charlie's cell there were outdated copies of newspapers and magazines, pull-out sections and everything else. It did all seem to make sense. I left Charlie to keep working on his scheme.

A week or so later, I looked into his cell again and he had a letter from the Home Office.

'Permission refused,' Charlie said, shrugging his shoulders.

'What? I suppose they must have had a good think about you and me starting a business in Parkhurst. We were both into organised crime, so they would have thought there had to be some skulduggery involved. I mean, they know you as the king of the long firm.'

Charlie lightened up. 'We ain't got permission in here, but we can start the business when we get out.'

It was a top idea. However, at that stage, I had no idea when or how we could get out. But I could see that, even in the early eighties, Charlie was years ahead with his business brain. They should have let him organise prison recycling.

Maybe the Home Office realised that. Before long, Charlie would have had the screws collecting all the waste paper while he took charge of the entire operation!

Our friendship grew and grew, and I noted that Charlie was a republican. He didn't like royalty or anything like that, so there was no chance of a picture of the Queen in his cell. I started to pop in to see him most days. On one occasion, he was sitting on his own, and the hot water for tea had just been delivered by a member of his firm. Charlie started pouring as soon as he saw me opening the door.

'I've been doing some thinking,' I said. 'You would have made a good prime minister.'

Charlie scoffed. 'I'm not that much of a crook.'

I chuckled at Charlie taking any opportunity to criticise politicians.

'Well, what I meant was that you have the brains to do it. You can build up a business from nothing, you know all about politicians and you can do *The Times* crossword in a few minutes.'

'Most of that is true,' Charlie nodded. 'Our problem is that we grew up on the wrong side of the fence. Crime was the only way to survive.'

Charlie became more serious and moved the conversation on to sit-downs and other protests. I was more than interested, with my escapade at Albany and a reputation as a troublemaker for most of my life.

'There was a huge riot here more than ten years ago, in the autumn of '69,' Charlie recalled. 'Frankie Fraser started it all. He was the ringleader. The screws were beating up some of the boys, so he organised a sit-down. Things got out of hand when they sent in a huge squad of screws from outside. They were all vicious and tooled up.

'Frankie spent a couple of days quietly telling everyone about his plans. Not everyone wanted to take part, so he gave them the option. That's fair because some of the boys were due to be released and they would have received more bird on top. If anyone was unwell he didn't press them, and people had others reasons as well.'

Charlie explained that, although plans were going well, Frankie encountered a major problem.

'Did someone grass?' I asked, using the word that was poison throughout the underworld.

'A Judas told one of the screws.'

'Who did that then?'

'Well, Frankie had his suspicions; I think there were a couple of grasses, actually. Frankie's main weapon was going to be surprise, and he lost that. Frankie said Ronnie Kray was being held down in the chokey at the time. Ronnie reported hearing two screws saying that they were going to get Frankie Fraser.'

'So they shipped prisoners out?'

Charlie looked angry as he continued with the story: 'Normally you would think they would have shipped out the organisers or segregated them. That's what you would have thought. Instead, they came in mob-handed from the mainland. There must have been 300 of them with their heavy-duty riot gear. They wanted a brutal confrontation to quash any idea of future riots. They could have found easy ways of avoiding trouble, but no ...

'Frank had planned his event for seven o'clock while people were having the association period. Around October, it would have been. Screws appeared from everywhere. They had advance warning, all right.'

'Brutal bastards,' I muttered.

'Many of the boys were beaten unconscious. Frankie was badly hurt, spent some time in hospital, and they gave him five years on top.'

'That won't put me off organising any protests in the future,' I assured him.

I told Charlie that, early on during my bird at Parkhurst, I made a protest and hoped it wouldn't affect my education plans. I felt I had to make a stand for everyone.

I made my own display of disgust about the rubbish food. It arrived from the kitchen, on its way to the hotplate, on a heated food trolley. The smell was bad enough. The prison food went off quickly, especially in the hot weather, and my nose told me something was wrong. I deliberately tipped the trolley over, and the grub and tea went everywhere. The screws were careful with me because they knew things could easily kick off. They were quite calm, negotiating and getting the chaps back into their cells.

I was banged up for a while, but I had stocked up on supplies from the canteen and I ate quite well. The tinned stuff tasted a lot better than the normal prison grub.

Another positive side was that they had to provide better food to prevent a full-scale riot. What normally happened, after the food trolley tipped over, was that they would send up improved meals that same day to keep everyone happy. Even cold meats and cheese were better alternatives to the horrible, overcooked veg.

'You've got a bit of form,' Charlie said. 'But they know you're clever, so let's hope they give you a new start with the Open University.'

I was now on good terms with the two main figures in Parkhurst. They both had their firms, with loyal supporters prepared to fight to the death. Charlie and Reggie commanded respect wherever they went in the prison; you could just sense their influence everywhere.

Charlie had the brains, and his quick mind could run rings round most people. Reggie was bright in his own way, although not half as sharp as Charlie. That would explain why the Richardsons made large sums from subtle, dodgy business dealings. The Krays appeared more as upfront gangsters, not so organised and drawing too much attention to themselves.

My head was, by now, full of ideas about going straight, improving my education and turning my life around. A long, difficult road lay ahead, but I sensed that one man held the key to my future: Charlie Richardson.

CHAPTER TWELVE

SAD NEWS FROM HOME

Visiting in Parkhurst took place in one big room. The visiting area was a separate brick building, away from the main prison and near the admin block. Most visiting rooms in prisons are not far from the front gates, meaning that any trouble can be contained some distance from the main prison buildings. They wouldn't want visitors getting near the wings and any sort of hostage situation developing.

You filled in a form, saying who you wanted to visit you. You would give names and addresses, and they would check the person out – who they associated with, background and everything. A form called a Visiting Order allowed the person to see you. You could have three visitors at a time, all carefully vetted.

Some people wouldn't be allowed to visit me if they seemed dodgy in any way. There were checks on computers to see if there was organised crime going on. If anything was picked up, your 'wished for' visitor went on a blacklist, with no chance of ever getting through the gates.

Parkhurst wasn't the easiest place to reach. A ferry ran from Southampton to Cowes, and there was the alternative of a ferry or hovercraft from Portsmouth to Ryde. After that, visitors took a taxi or bus to Newport in the centre of the Isle of Wight. Then they walked down Clissold Road with that dark, grim, red-bricked monstrosity of Parkhurst towering over them.

My brothers and sisters were keen visitors, despite the expense. For a start, they had to drive from London to Southampton. If the weather turned nasty they couldn't catch the ferry and had to stay in a hotel for a night or two – that could cost them a couple of hundred quid. They came to see me every few weeks, in any case, always two-handed. No one ever came alone.

I suggested that they didn't need to come so often, and also that it wasn't a good idea to bring their children. Although the kids were grown up, it was bad for them to see the grim surroundings.

You could save your visits and store them up. That meant your family could spend the weekend on the island and visit on both the Saturday and the Sunday. Because of the expense and the difficulty getting there, some prisoners received hardly any visits. I was grateful to my close friends and family for making the effort.

Visitors often complained about a not-too-friendly welcome from the prison officers in reception. There were forms to sign. The screws carried out body searches for cigarettes, cash, weapons and, of course, drugs. A photo ID was needed and also proof of address. There was little or no conversation with the screws; visitors were almost made to feel guilty of committing an offence themselves!

After a wait while the details were double checked, the temporary arrivals were marched down a series of corridors to a large visiting hall. They could see yellowing paint on the walls, strip lights beating down even in the heat of summer, and very basic chairs alongside Formica tables.

Sometimes you sat down at a table and your people came across to you. But other times they were already at the table, so you went over to them.

We had our own communications network. Someone might pass on information to a wife. All the wives knew each other and news would spread like wildfire. It was more effective than BT. There were no crossed lines. If someone was moved prison, we would have all the details by the next day at least, and sometimes even on the same day.

The IRA also had their own methods, and they managed to keep tabs on friend or foe. It was obviously more difficult for the IRA men to receive visits because their families had to come from Northern Ireland. The prison officers gave special attention to anyone visiting the IRA men. Because many of the screws were ex-servicemen, their passion for the searches came as no surprise.

There were no glass partitions, telephones or anything much apart from the tables. It was usually only when you were on remand that areas were sectioned off.

At Parkhurst you had about an hour for the visit. Screws sat at another table or they walked up and down. Most of the people who came to the island were family and friends. They were mainly straightgoers.

If someone vaguely suspicious came to see you, the screws watched closely and tried to listen to what was going on. When a famous person visited Reggie Kray, they would check everything about the visitor and who he or she was associated with.

Although I was in prison, I still managed to control quite a bit of business in the manor. If money could be smuggled in to me, then it would be added to my lending capital.

Protection rackets were still going on. I would make suggestions, through coded letters and meeting visitors, as to how things should proceed. For example, I might be asked for guidance on how a restaurant should be offered protection.

I would suggest a name to go along and talk to the owner, and make it clear that there would be no trouble for so many readies a week – several hundred pounds, maybe. We could even provide a doorman. Of course, if our services weren't required, there could be unwanted trouble at the club, with police called and all sorts of aggro. It was always better to take our advice in these matters.

During a typical visit, a friend, usually a straight-goer, would have a message for me that 'so and so' was causing trouble in our area. He might be smashing things up in a pub, being loud and aggressive or generally out of order. I would issue an instruction to clump him or, in other words, to deliver a right hander. If I thought that a strong punch wasn't enough, I would say he should be cut with a blade. In extreme cases, a worse fate lay in store.

During the next visit, I would receive confirmation that the problem had been sorted.

'He's been cut. He's learned his lesson. He won't be back on the manor.'

Another time I might receive a letter, simply saying that the favour I asked for had been carried out. And all of this was prompted by a visit from a pal.

All sorts of matters were resolved during visits. In the exercise yard you would have chatted to your mates. All the faces from the wings gathered together. The screws didn't like that because they knew we were discussing business, bits of work or whether someone had to be sorted out. One of your pals might say a rat had done a wrong 'un, like grassed on someone, and was being moved to another nick like Coldingley in Surrey.

'I know someone in Coldingley,' you would hear one of the chaps saying. So this chap would be told, when his old woman came on a visit, to pass on the message about the rat. The contact in Coldingley would make sure the rat was 'served up' … or, in other words, cut up. They would really give it to him.

I often saw Reggie at one of the tables, greeting his visitors. His older brother, Charlie Kray, used to come along with some close pals. Reg usually wore a grey tracksuit and white plimsolls. And, as always, he was accompanied by three tough-looking young guys. They all had fair hair and blue eyes. These were the young prisoners who carried out Reg's cleaning duties – and also acted as his protectors.

The young minders were, apparently, all 'tooled-up' with weapons – though, of course, you couldn't see what they were carrying. The protectors were there in case any prisoner or visitor wanted to make a name for himself. In such a violent, intimidating atmosphere, that was always a possibility.

I knew that attempts were made to smuggle drugs into Reg. He never used drugs but, in prison, they were a highly valuable currency. In exchange for them, Reg could get any favours he wanted – and any jobs carried out for him.

Conversation was never easy. I could see that Reg had difficulty hearing what his visitors had to say. His eyes were constantly darting around the room, always looking for danger. Occasionally a fight would break out between two prisoners at adjoining tables – or between a con and his wife or partner. The prison officers would pounce within seconds.

Charlie Kray was no stranger to me. As well as seeing him visiting at Parkhurst, I'd also got to know him very well when he was doing his bird at various prisons in the past. I spent a couple of years with him at Maidstone when I was in for manslaughter. Charlie was a tragic case, really. He was nothing like his brothers at all, but he adored them and they thought the world of him.

Charlie was one of the loveliest men you could meet. He used to have long hair in those days. He was always pleasant, never rude to anyone and I noticed that he behaved like a gentleman.

Despite his protests, Charlie was found guilty of being an accessory to the murder of Jack 'The Hat' McVitie. He was released in 1975 and sorted out the twins' business interests.

The problem facing Charlie: he was a Kray. He was one of the brothers so he was classed alongside them. Charlie was never in the same league as a criminal. He tried to smooth things over, but the twins were both out of their nuts and he couldn't cool them down.

He was just born into a bad lot. When Reg and Ron were little, he spent most of his time looking after them. Then, when they got older, he taught them to box. When they got out of control, he had to take a step back.

Charlie Kray didn't agree with what they were doing, but they were his brothers and blood is thicker than water. He was just caught up with those two. He wasn't straight, obviously. He was ducking and diving with his own scams after the McVitie case, but not on the scale of the twins.

If anyone said a bad word about Charlie Kray, the twins would have cut them to pieces. He tried to keep well away from the killings and the more serious business.

Even Reggie told me: 'Charlie would never let us down. He's our brother. But he's never fitted in with what we're doing. He doesn't have the bite or the killer instinct. He does what he does and we do what we do.'

When I saw Charlie Kray visiting Reggie, I knew most things about both of the brothers. I suppose I saw Charlie on both sides of the fence, as a prisoner and a visitor. It was a shame that such a talented man had to spend so much time within the prison system for whatever reason; Charlie could have made much more use of his business skills.

The visits from my family were the highlights of my spell in Parkhurst. In mid-1982, though, my world collapsed.

'Vera, thanks so much for coming. You know it means a lot to me.'

My sister, three years older than me and the second youngest in the family, was sitting at a table in the visiting room. She was tiny, like Mum, and beautiful with her blonde hair and blue eyes. She had already been searched by a screw. I did wonder where my brother Freddy was.

'He's outside having a smoke. He'll come in later. I've got something to tell you. I wanted to tell you myself. It's about Mum.'

'Just tell me how it is,' I insisted, as that was my normal way with no beating around the bush.

'Mum has leukaemia.'

I could feel my eyes filling with tears. I had let her down so much and, now when I wanted to see her, I couldn't do a thing. I felt totally helpless. I was close to Mum and Vera, and I appreciated my sister's insistence on seeing me alone for a bit.

'She is getting treatment,' Vera said, hopefully.

A couple of minutes' silence followed. My mum was only sixty-five. I thought about her, tidying around the house. She was so tiny, our mum, only five-foot-two with dark brown hair and glasses. We all did little jobs to help her. I polished the shoes, Vera did the washing up and the others tackled various chores. We just mucked in.

Every time any of us walked into the house we would kiss and cuddle our mum. We used to show her a lot of affection.

'I hope you're being good?' she always asked me, not realising what I was up to with my life of crime.

'Of course, Mum,' I answered, not able to tell her. I never brought any sort of weapon into the house and kept my operations secret.

Mum was a great fan of the Queen Mother. Like Dad, she used to watch the royal family on TV when she could. If the Queen Mother wore blue, Dad would go out and buy a blue outfit for Mum, so she had a dress in the same colour for special occasions.

After a tearful Vera left the visiting room, replaced by Freddy, I thought more about Mum and how I had kept her away from the visiting routine. She only visited once in jail, when I was remand at Brixton. It was a total disaster. She had to go through all the security and searching. Mum had never even had a bag searched in her life before, so it was a horrendous ordeal.

'Bobby, what's happening here?' she whispered, bursting into tears.

'It's all right, Mum, I'm fine. I just have to get through this and then I'll be back home as soon as I can.'

I told my family that Mum should never visit me at Brixton again. I was looking at a trial with maybe up to a thirty-year sentence. I knew I was going down for a big 'un. That was hard enough to sort out in my head. I needed to be surrounded by tough people who understood the rules. I couldn't say in front of Mum that someone needed to be shot. Maybe a grass had to be dealt with, but I couldn't let her know any of that.

I said to my family: 'This is too upsetting for Mum. Keep her away. She doesn't understand anything about prison or villains. Never bring her here again.'

In the Parkhurst visiting room, Freddy knew that Vera had told me everything. A couple of screws edged nearer to see if were talking business. That couldn't have been further from the truth. As the two of us sat, monitored by screws, we drifted back in time.

'I remember your first real bit of work and Mum's reaction,' Freddy said, reflecting on some difficult periods in our past lives. 'Mum got very upset. Was that when you held up the geezers at a youth club?'

'Yeah, we robbed some guys who drove a delivery van. Mum just cried and cried. Dad knew what I had been up to and demanded that I should never lie to him. We'd used a hacksaw to cut down the size of a shotgun. The gun belonged to the dad of one of my pals. We only got about £6 from the raid after holding people up, so it was a total disaster.'

'The Old Bill were looking everywhere for you that night,' Freddy said.

'They caught up with me and there was no way I could avoid telling Mum,' I recalled. 'It's hard to believe that I was walking around, carrying a shotgun, at the age of sixteen.'

Freddy, now free after doing his time, sat totally still as I reflected on everything I'd done.

'You'll also remember I sometimes stayed at home, and then moved between houses to stay on the move. My crazy life affected her too much, especially after Dad died. I'll just keep writing to her from here and pray she gets better. I'm relieved she never saw me in here, surrounded by all these cons and screws.'

Mum kept writing to me, despite her illness, with general chit-chat about what was going on at home and wondering if I was being good. She even said that her bank manager was asking after me; this amused me, as I'd robbed that particular bank, so maybe he was wondering how long I had left of my sentence!

I wrote back, asking her to stay strong and to get well. A typical letter would say the weather was nice and sunny although we'd just had rain. I said what a nice place the Isle of Wight was, with the seaside and beaches. I could hardly tell her the latest stories about Parkhurst's murderers and lunatics. I tried to think of things to say that might lift her spirits.

My sister Pauline was given paintings, from an unexpected source, to take back to Mum. Reggie Kray and Ronnie did a couple of a caravan and some flowers – Ronnie had arranged for his work to be sent down from Broadmoor. Pauline, another beauty with her blonde hair and blue eyes, thought they were awful.

'Bobby, these are terrible. I've got to go on the ferry with them. Could you tell your friends they're too heavy to carry or something?'

Mum told Pauline: 'I can't understand why these boys are in prison when they send me so many lovely things. I'm always getting presents from Reggie Kray. Isn't that nice?'

I heard that one of the paintings was so bad that Pauline hid it behind a wardrobe.

Visiting did help me to visualise a light at the end of the tunnel. It had a positive impact on me. Instead of talking to other faces and screws, I was able to chat to my family and friends, catching up on news from the outside.

Sitting in the visiting room at Parkhurst, with my loved ones within touching distance, I latched onto hope; one day, I believed, I would be free and able to enjoy my new life with them.

I knew, unlike many people in there, that day would eventually come. I also knew that one particular visit from my brother and sister had dealt me a devastating blow. I was facing the loss of the most important person in my life – my mum.

CHAPTER THIRTEEN

GOOD AND
BAD SCREWS

'Hey, Bobby, would you like an apple?'

'Yes, please,' I answered, still under the weather because of the sad news from home.

A bleak, grey day in Parkhurst was brightened up by the sight of Foxy, the PO – Principal Officer – on 'B' wing, walking around carrying a brown sack filled with apples. He was in his late fifties or early sixties, and had silvery grey hair and glasses. Portly, with quite a bit of meat on him, he talked with a strong Hampshire accent mixed with a flavour of the Isle of Wight. It was English, but not as I knew it, with occasional words I'd never heard before.

'I heard a couple of the other warders talking about your mum. Your sister must have told them to make sure you were okay.'

'Well, it's not good, Foxy, but I'll just have to keep doing my bird and hope that she survives.'

'Leukaemia does go into remission. I've heard of people lasting years with the treatment nowadays.'

Foxy was doing his best to cheer me up. I had a few loans and deals to arrange, although I hardly felt like doing anything at all. I could see that he was going to change the conversation and try to boost my spirits. I did relish the chance to enjoy a small luxury like a fresh rosy apple.

'I got them from a local orchard. Nice and firm and crunchy, they are. I thought I would give the grockles a treat today.'

'Grockles? You're having a laugh? What the fuck is a grockle?'

'Well, it's usually a tourist or a visitor. I suppose I could call you a visitor, although you might be on an extended stay depending on behaviour. It's an old word on the island, and there are plenty more where that came from. Maybe you're really an overnor.'

'An overnor? Did you say overnor or governor?'

'An overnor is someone from the mainland who's settled on the island,' Foxy went on, enjoying himself. 'Maybe you could qualify there. But you're definitely not a caulkhead.'

'Caulkhead? You're having me on. Nobody has ever called me a caulkhead before. I hope it ain't insulting.'

Foxy was in his element: 'A caulkhead is someone who was born on the island, into a well-established family here.'

Foxy switched back to the subject he could see was still troubling me, 'You must be anxious about your mum as you're a bit helpless in here.'

'I'm waiting for news from my sister, Vera. I need to get hold of her.'

'Come into the office,' Foxy gestured. 'Use the phone.'

There is good in everyone, so they say, and to be fair there were some decent screws in Parkhurst.

I felt humble. An armed robber with a formidable record was being shown genuine kindness here. I nodded my appreciation, went into Foxy's office, made my call, got a quick update on Mum's condition from my sister and shook the officer by the hand.

'Better news. She's not bad at all today. People do go up and down with cancer.'

'Keep me posted,' Foxy smiled.

'You do know you're called Foxy,' I grinned as I walked back out onto the landing. 'I heard the boys talking about you.'

'Well, the name is Fox, but everyone does call me Foxy. Maybe I'm more like a silver fox. I don't mind the nickname.'

I felt a rush of respect, despite my status as a hardened, ruthless armed robber. 'I'm heading back to the cell to listen to the radio. Thanks for looking after me.'

The great thing about Foxy was that he talked like a human being. He had a knack of calming people down and making them feel a lot better. His remedies worked for me. Foxy was a psychologist, a social worker and prison officer all rolled into one. He could have walked into the middle of a riot and no one would have hurt him.

The guy really cared. When I was pretending to do my cleaning duties – undertaken by Reggie's boys – he would leave biscuits out for me. I used to share them with the other Cat 'A' cleaners who weren't doing any cleaning either.

'He's a decent bloke,' we all agreed as we munched on a plate of assorted treats. 'He's far too good for here.'

Only a couple of weeks after helping me with the phone call, I heard that Foxy had been taken ill and died. A lot of the chaps were upset. We arranged for some flowers to go to the funeral as a mark of respect.

Many of the screws were taking tranquilisers because they lived on the edge. Anything could kick off at any time; they could be attacked without warning. I'm sure Foxy toughed it out without pills.

Then there was John, an ordinary Parkhurst landing screw who looked like a tubby Captain Birdseye. He had fair hair and a fair beard that seemed to take over his entire head. He would have made a good Viking warrior.

'No ferries this week,' John boomed along the landing. 'The weather's a bastard on the Solent. It's blowin' a hooley out there.'

That meant no visitors, of course, making us all feel totally marooned, just for a change, on the island. I remembered with affection Foxy's word, 'grockle'.

Whatever you called them, no one was going anywhere that day.

'Bad news,' I muttered with a glum expression. 'And I'm a bit short of snout.'

'Here,' John offered, opening his tobacco tin.

John knew it was near to pay day, so we were running short of supplies, while he had an ample source on the outside. We only received a couple of quid a week to spend on luxuries, meaning that John's tin was a welcome sight.

He was fascinated about my background and life of crime. 'How do you go about killing people?' John asked. It was the last thing I expected him to say.

I hesitated before I answered, as I had a life of crime behind me and possibly some grey areas not to be mentioned.

'Well, I killed one person, but it was an accident and I went down for manslaughter a few years ago.'

'Yes, but all these gangland murders in London. I heard you had been a hitman. Did you work as a hitman?'

'I can't tell you everything I'm supposed to have done,' I explained. 'There are a few hitmen around. I just got done for armed robberies. Being a hitman is just a bit of work.'

'A bit of work?'

'It's business.'

'How do you work that one out?'

A hitman in the sixties and seventies didn't accept a contract from just anyone. He would be contacted to see if he was up for the job. The contract would have to be offered by a respected member of a firm, whose roots could be traced back at least three generations. If the police arrested him, he could be banged up for ever, but he would never grass.

'You're trained professionally by an ex-Army geezer or a gun expert,' I told John. 'Maybe someone is coming into the manor causing trouble or trying to muscle in on your territory. He has to be taken out. The victim has to be seen as vermin or something to get rid of, not as a human being.'

John's mouth gaped open.

'You have to check out the geezer's daily habits, when he walks his dog, when he's vulnerable and everything like that. You can't whack him in front of his wife and family, that's not on, so you wait for the right time.'

'That's horrible stuff,' John said, screwing up his face.

'In my world, that's how it is. A hitman gets paid, just like a normal worker.'

'Are the people always killed with a gun?'

'No, it's when the hitman gets the opportunity. Someone could be run over, suffocated or strangled. A lot of the killings are made to look like accidents. A diabetic might accidentally overdose on insulin – the hitman would have organised that, but it would really look like an accident. If someone had a heart condition, the hitman would find a way of tampering with his medication. It's all totally professional in our business.'

John shook his head: 'I have to say, Bobby, I've never heard anything like that in my life. It's another world. I thought these hits were done in the street from motor-bikes or cars?'

'Yeah, you're talking about an execution in public. You're right, a bike would pull up and the geezer would be shot in the head. It would be a message to another firm to get out of town or watch what they were doing. I've heard of other cases where the body was cut up and a message sent to a firm in another way.'

'Another way?'

'Yeah, an eye would be delivered to the firm. The eye could only come from their man.'

I told John that I was always at risk in the mid-seventies because of inter-gang rivalry. I was shot in the leg with a hunting rifle and cut open with a carpet knife. When the rifle fired, I was walking along the street. The .22 bullet felt red hot when it hit me, and the pain was horrendous. It went straight through my leg. I was fortu-nate because I was told later that it was a hair's breadth away from my kneecap.

And I was targeted with a shotgun. The lights went down on a motor, the window opened and BANG. That one missed and some of the pellets hit a member of our firm, Big Eddie. Still, he was able to chase after the car and smash in a window. We couldn't go to any hospital, with the police getting involved, so we used an ex-Army geezer who'd worked as a medic. The people involved in both shootings were 'educated', as we called it, so you can imagine what happened to them.

John opened his mouth wide again and retreated into his office. The inquisitive screw had heard enough for one day.

I knew all about how hitmen in the seventies operated, down to the finest detail. One geezer walked out of a police station on bail. A gun appeared and he was whacked at close range. A motorcycle in dim light, with the rider wearing black leathers, isn't the easiest to trace.

You read about hitmen in books and magazines. The writers don't know what it is like to put a gun barrel in someone's mouth, fire a shot at kneecaps or actually take a life. That is why people have asked me over the years about the life of a hitman. Because I know.

Not everyone can become a hitman. A thug is a thug. He could be a bouncer, but never a cold-blooded assassin. All he can do is use muscle to eject someone from a club. He's not highly trained with weapons and would probably have no interest anyway. I could never be a doorman, but someone like me would have no problems being a hitman.

Even in the world of the hitman, there is black humour. A club doorman was approached and asked if he could get hold of rounds for a particular gun. The weapon itself was easy to come by – but the hitman needed the right ammunition. The club doorman knew an underworld contact who could make rounds up himself. So that was no problem.

The hitman came back, not knowing who the target was, and collected the bullets to carry out his contract.

About a week later the potential assassin returned with the ammunition and sheepishly handed over the bullets. The intended victim was the doorman himself! The hitman decided not to take up the contract, and a life was saved under bizarre circumstances.

In Parkhurst there was another John, a Senior Officer or SO, who had worked directly under the late Foxy. We called him Johnny. He was in his forties and laid back – a younger version of Foxy, really. He sorted out the rotas and that sort of thing. It was obvious that he had been trained by Foxy and shown how to perform. He got on well with the boys, talking about football and rugby.

Above the SO and PO we had Chief Officers, who were later replaced by Assistant Governors in suits.

Some of the screws became wing officers, making them feel good, while new recruits would take their place on the landings.

The chaps used to take the piss out of the wing officers: 'You're just normal screws. Are you commissioned officers? Should we call you "sir"?'

That really hacked them off. The jumped-up screws were frothing at the mouth.

All of the screws hated it when someone topped himself. You can imagine them coming into a cell and seeing a geezer hanging there. They knew that, shortly afterwards, tensions would rise and everyone would get edgy. They tried to keep everything calm; generally, the screws were looking for a quiet life. Rather than use heavy-handed treatment, they would talk to you when things kicked off.

Screws in the hospital wing at Parkhurst were always a bit iffy. You never knew what lay in wait for you there. They could dope you up for no reason, or you could go in with a broken leg and they could give you an aspirin. It was as if the hospital screws were on another little planet. They were nasty and just had no feelings. You had to watch what you said in that hospital wing. They could decide that you were too violent and had a screw loose, and should be 'nutted off' to Broadmoor like Ronnie Kray.

One screw who didn't understand the Parkhurst regime was ginger, skinny and in his late thirties. We called him Gold Top. He was a bit thick and only worked there for a couple of months before he had to be transferred. He was totally useless. He had no idea how the regime operated and nearly got hurt. He was trying to be the boss, but he should have known better. We heard that he'd been a milkman, so the nickname Gold Top suited him perfectly.

Gold Top had probably been to a local nick where he could order everybody about – screws and cons. In Parkhurst, that didn't work. There were severe nutters in the place who could carve you up if you were a screw or an inmate. They weren't getting out so they didn't care.

'Bang up, bang up,' Gold Top hissed as he tried to get everyone into their cells for the night.

'Fuck off, Gold Top,' everybody laughed. 'Just fuck off.'
Even the sensible screws enjoyed the entertainment.

Gold Top couldn't count. That proved to be a major obstacle for the useless twat, who was more used to counting milk crates. When the prisoners came back from exercise, he had to count them all in. He kept messing up the numbers, so they gave him a plastic clicker thing. One prisoner, one click. The next person, another click.

What an opportunity for a wind-up. People would go in, go back out and come in again. Then they would come in mob handed, go out and in again. He was clicking like mad, with no hope of getting it right. They got shot of Gold Top, lively.

While I was at Parkhurst, some of the screws were smuggling cannabis into the building. Don't forget that the screws didn't earn a lot, and drugs in prisons in my day were worth a small fortune. A bent screw mixed with people who he knew weren't going to shop him. If you shopped someone in there, you were dead.

It started off with a friendly warder bringing in some tobacco. Then he was 'open'. After that, some beer might appear along with a bottle of whisky.

As a reward, the screw didn't receive cash or have to carry money around. He would be told about the benefits of his cooperation. 'We've got a villa in Spain. You can go across with your family for a couple of weeks and it won't cost you a penny. It's all laid on.'

There was little chance of getting caught, while the compensation for his efforts was substantial. When you pay people crap wages and ask them to take maximum risks, they will look for another way of earning money. That's what you're talking about here. Someone would offer them a better deal for their families. They were talking to chaps with Rolls-Royces and places in America, and people who were used to going to all the top casinos.

The screws put drugs to good use during those times when the weather halted the ferries. With no visitors arriving, the prisoners had to be kept calm. All of a sudden, cannabis appeared on the wing. Where did that come from, then? There was no powder or anything like that, but the puff was doing the rounds.

It could only have come from the screws, and they had confiscated the gear in the first place. The staff didn't want things kicking off. Riots could cause thousands – even millions – of pounds worth of damage, with people hurt and headlines in the newspapers. Everyone needed to be calmed down, pacified and sedated. Then, when the weather eased up, visitors did the sneaking of drugs into the prison and the screws could concentrate on their day jobs.

The odd screw smoked puff, too. Imagine dealing with people like the Yorkshire Ripper every day. They needed to calm down a lot. It was like working in a lunatic asylum.

The bottom line was that some screws were smuggling in puff, and so were the prisoners. The screws must have known that catapults were being used to fire drugs over the wall. Someone on the outside would put an ounce of puff in a parcel. They would find a spot and a time when a camera wasn't pointing in their direction, and fire the parcel over the wall. A geezer would be cleaning the yard with a brush – his job was to pick up the parcel and deliver it to the prisoner, waiting for his delivery on the wing.

The screws must also have had an idea that, if a cassette player arrived on the wing, it might not just be a case of someone liking Lionel Richie or another star of the period. It would be full of LSD tablets. So the guy received his tablets then sold them on the wing.

Screws monitored the post. However, an ingenious method was used to hoodwink them. A letter was soaked in LSD and allowed to dry out. The loved one or whoever then wrote on the letter, 'Dear Harry' and all the usual romantic stuff. Once the letter was received, it could be cut up into small squares and sold for a fiver a pop. LSD could also be put under the stamp, giving someone quite a trip when they received their letter.

Another older warder, known as Jimbo, was an alcoholic. I never knew his real name. He drank off duty and would have loved to have a tipple on duty, too, given half a chance. Jimbo would have been about five-foot-ten, but he looked shorter because of a stoop. He had some sort of back problem and leaned quite a bit. He was probably only in his forties but looked much older because of his drinking habits, and had a heavily lined face with a shaven head and bulging, bloodshot eyes.

A boozy opportunity arose for Jimbo over Christmas, but not how he expected. Every few days we brewed our own brand of hooch in a cell as far from the screws as possible, using whatever was available from the kitchen.

The traditional method of making hooch involved sugar, fruit and maybe potato peelings, yeast and those large containers normally used for liquid soap. There were a few expert brewers; I watched and admired their skills of manufacture and concealment.

The smell had to be disguised. A lot of gas came from the sugar and yeast. Overall, the aroma resembled rotting apples. It was a horrible stench, and the hooch makers tried hard to keep the screws off the scent. All sorts of methods were employed, including aftershave, talcum powder or even that smelly stuff sports people use on their muscles.

The best way was to move the hooch around so as not to contaminate individual cells. The whiff was spread around the wing while everyone tried to disguise the smell. This went on for around three weeks, and I am sure the screws pretended not to notice, knowing that we were keeping out of trouble and concentrating on the brewing.

Once it was strained off, the party could begin. And those were some parties. Radios played pop music, we laughed and joked, people were sick all over the place and somehow survived the horrendous after-effects of the semi-poisonous hooch. I enjoyed the atmosphere but rarely touched the stuff!

On one occasion, we attracted Jimbo's attention. He was fascinated as we worked on our highly illegal pick-me-up. We just assumed that he would turn a blind eye and get on with his work.

Perhaps Jimbo's nostrils told him that our creation was about to be unleashed on the wing. Maybe he heard the chatter as the boys prepared to celebrate the festive season with some low-grade booze in low-grade, chipped mugs. We chose the cell occupied by a nutter called Lennie the Lid as it was furthest away from the screws' office.

About eight o'clock, we had a happy little gathering, mainly London armed robbers. The Police, not the Old Bill variety, blared from a pop station on my radio. The song was 'Message in a Bottle', causing hilarity as we imagined sending out an SOS from the island via the waters of the Solent.

As we were about to pour, Jimbo appeared in a flash: 'What does it taste like? Can I try some? What's in it?'

I thought the ingredients might put him off. 'We got various odds and ends from the kitchen like potato peelings and mixed it with yeast and a couple of secret ingredients. It's ready now.'

'Hold up a minute, a mug for Jimbo,' I ordered.

An IRA hand produced a mug in reasonable nick, filled to the brim with our foaming hooch. Jimbo accepted the mug, had a good sniff, a glug around his mouth and then a full-hearted swallow. We re-filled the screw's mug several times and he enjoyed every drop, making enthusiastic slurping noises.

Then, panic stations. A clatter of footsteps. Voices on the landing. Trouble!

In a flash, Jimbo dived under the bed, while the others slipped all the evidence under there with him. I produced a couple of books, and sat on top of Lennie's bed while the assembled group pretended to be reading and listening to the radio.

After the all-clear, we had a look under the bed. Jimbo was snoring away, still clutching the mug of hooch. He was blind drunk. In the morning, we gave a heads up to a friendly screw, who organised a smuggling operation to sneak Jimbo home.

Good screws, bad screws, druggy screws, boozy screws. I encountered them all at Parkhurst!

CHAPTER FOURTEEN

A TIME FOR LEARNING

Books, books and more books. Charlie's influence meant that I became addicted to learning. I was getting about six books a week from the library. Charlie encouraged me to read about a range of subjects from sociology to the history of the Isle of Wight. I was even keen on finding out more about his favourite subject: minerals and all that game.

I went across to the education area and chose from the books already there or ordered what I needed. To be fair, Parkhurst provided a good service. There was no way out of Britain's Alcatraz and its surroundings; I was keen to find out everything I could about my island home. The prison's past certainly went some way towards me wanting to go straight!

The local writers in the newspapers told me that the Isle of Wight itself is hardly a frightening place. The ferries arrive at Ryde and Cowes, both pleasant places beside the water. Parkhurst is inland a bit, near the town of Newport. There's a large forest beside Parkhurst, including a substantial area of ancient woodland – not for the inquisitive eyes of prisoners, though.

Cowes is famous for the annual sailing regatta. It's the oldest and biggest in the world. Cowes Week is always at the start of August and attracts hundreds of racing yachts. I've never been a sailor myself, but I read there are usually 8,000 yachts and 100,000 people watching.

On the final Friday of Cowes Week, there's a spectacular firework display. A book about the history of Cowes Week told me all I needed to know, with no chance of getting a glimpse of the action. I found that frustrating. The desire to experience freedom became a raging flame inside me.

I read up about Queen Victoria's holiday home, Osborne House. Now that did really interest me, being a royalist. Osborne House isn't far from where the sailing events happen at Cowes. Queen Victoria's nine children, including Edward VII, the future king, learned to swim in the sea there and spent much of their time gathering shells from the shoreline.

After the Queen's death, the mansion became a convalescent home for the military and a training college for the Royal Navy.

On a much smaller scale, I read about a model village in Godshill. It's set in the grounds of the Old Vicarage.

There are scale models of local villages as they were in the 1920s, all a tenth the size of real life. I also saw pictures in the local newspaper. I imagined a great day out as a free man. Even the tiny trees and shrubs are manicured to perfection.

I found it quite bizarre are that all of this excitement was almost within touching distance, and yet I was locked up in dismal surroundings, with a vague hope of release, well into the future.

I learned, through the library, that the Parkhurst story began almost exactly 200 years before my incarceration there. Two centuries ago, this bleak, bleak place – a scar on the landscape – showed not even the tiniest amount of compassion.

A military hospital with an asylum was established in 1778. Parkhurst Barracks, later Albany Barracks, opened twenty years later. In 1807, soldiers were based there, training for the Peninsular War as Britain, Spain and Portugal took on the might of Napoleon.

In 1838, the bleak building became a prison for children. 'Parkhurst Apprentices', or 'Parkhurst Boys' as they were called, were transported to Australia and New Zealand for committing petty crimes. They weren't armed robbers like me; more likely they'd stolen a loaf of bread to feed the family.

Young children had to wait several weeks, alongside hardened criminals, before the case came to trial. It was not uncommon for a child, accused of stealing a bottle of milk, to wait seven weeks for the case to be heard. And that kid could be as young as ten. Girls were also treated harshly. Instead of transportation, they were sentenced to hard labour.

The boys who had been condemned to transportation were housed in a young offenders' wing. They were taught a trade, provided with some education and sent off into the dangerous unknown to serve the remaining years of their sentence.

The records speak for themselves. George Barker, fourteen, was sent to Western Australia on board the convict ship, *Cumberland*, for stealing a shawl. The sentence of seven years' transportation was handed out at Norwich Sessions.

The *Cumberland* left the Isle of Wight on 30 September 1845. After four gruelling months at sea, she arrived in Fremantle. Her cargo: twenty-five passengers and twelve Parkhurst Boys. Other regular convict ships included the *Simon Taylor, Shepherd, Halifax, Orient, Ameer* and *Mary*.

When George arrived he became a farm servant, then a miller's lad. He was jailed for absconding, but after that 'was doing pretty well'. He fell short of expectations during a spell as a shepherd; his master reported that he was 'subject to dysentery, indolent and loses sheep'.

Bristol Sessions convicted fifteen-year-old Richard Bell to seven years' transportation in 1846 for stealing five pounds of fat. A previous conviction had to be taken into consideration, although the records don't say if he was a persistent thief of fat. Again, the role of farm servant and shepherd lay in wait and, after a disappointing report of 'sullen and idle', he was 'very much improved'.

Tragedy, though, lay in wait for Richard Andrews, thirteen, who was convicted of a felony at Surrey Sessions. As usual, the boy was prepared for the gruelling voyage at Parkhurst. His master 'down under', A. Cornish, reported that Richard was 'a very good boy' who received excellent reports. He was killed 'by the upsetting of a cart he was driving. He had long borne an excellent character and his death was sincerely regretted by his master.'

William Bickle from Devonport was only eleven when he arrived at Parkhurst. He also received seven years' transportation for stealing a watch.

William was sent to Point Puer, Tasmania. His behaviour was described as 'troublesome', earning him lashes, solitary confinement and an extra two years on top of his sentence. The bewildered William had to join an adult work gang and spent a month on a treadmill. Not only that, he was forced to endure twelve months' hard labour in chains. In 1843, William was freed, and is now remembered in Tasmania's Port Arthur Visitor Centre.

John Lynch was deported at the age of nine for stealing toys. His prison record states that he was reprimanded for laughing in a chapel. It's hard to believe that another two children, only six and eight years old, were brutally whipped for stealing a cash box.

After leaving Parkhurst, the young boys endured horrendous conditions aboard convict ships. The youngsters suffered from seasickness, measles, scurvy, dysentery, typhoid and cholera. They were taken on board in chains, which were unlocked once on the ship. The convicts were taken to the prison deck below, and the hatch was locked.

The only respite was occasional fresh air and exercise on the deck.

The lash was in constant use for those who misbehaved. Any more nonsense on board and the hapless young man was placed in a box too small to stand up in.

Conditions on the ships did gradually improve as education and religious instruction were brought in. Also, bonuses were paid for the safe landing of the prisoners – and so the Parkhurst Boys benefited from the changes.

Between 1842 and 1852, 1,500 boys left Parkhurst for Australia, New Zealand, Tasmania, and a tiny outpost in the Pacific called Norfolk Island.

After their seven years of hell, most of the young kids stayed in Australia, joining free settlers. Some of them even rose to lofty positions in the country. Many Australians were ashamed by this heritage until well into the twentieth century. Now, a convict ancestor is more likely to be a source of pride in a carefully researched family tree.

The first arrivals in New Zealand in 1842 were not so welcome. The 3,000 settlers in Auckland were trying to forge a living for themselves, without the need for a boatload of young kids from Parkhurst. Around 130 boys settled in Auckland where they eventually found friends – the Maori. The names of Parkhurst Boys live on in their communities to this day.

Back on the Isle of Wight, pointless tasks were prepared for young children who had not been sentenced to transportation. Many were forced to spend six hours at a time on a treadmill, which served no purpose other than to punish the kid.

The crank was another pointless machine. The young prisoner turned a handle, moving gravel around in a box. In some prisons, the crank had to be turned until late at night before any food would be provided. Anyone who failed to turn the crank properly faced the prospect of being strapped to the wall in a straitjacket for several hours. Buckets of water were thrown on children as young as ten if they dared to pass out.

Although I had a tough time in prisons as a youth and young man, I winced as I read that children, not yet in their teens, could be hit with a birch rod or whipped up to twenty-four times in one session. How could that happen? And there I was, in the same building, possibly near the spot where the punishments had been handed out.

In 1847, prisoners built a wing at Parkhurst, digging the clay and baking the bricks. Parkhurst became a female prison in 1863. Six years later, it became a jail for male offenders, and stayed that way.

The hospital at Parkhurst was established as a separate four-storey building with four wards and around forty single cells. It even boasted an operating theatre.

In 1968, Parkhurst became one of the first dispersal prisons for maximum security prisoners like me. As I saw, dangerous prisoners were ghosted around the various jails, rather than settling in too long and causing trouble in any one place.

Albany Barracks was used by the British Army until 1960, catering mainly for infantry regiments.

Albany was built as a Category 'C' training prison on the same site in the early sixties. Shortly afterwards came an upgrade to Category 'B' and then in 1970 the jail became part of the dispersal system.

And, a few years after that, I arrived along with a selection of the country's most dangerous people. Like me, they were violent, dangerous and unpredictable.

Prisons in the eighties had moved on leaps and bounds since the bad old days, although there was still room for major improvements. I was beginning to see that training schemes or rehabilitation programmes were needed to stop people returning to places like Parkhurst.

As far as I could see, Charlie and I made most use of the library and any courses on offer. Other faces came and went, but we were dedicated. And I couldn't get enough books on history, English and sociology.

'Education will keep you out of here, when you've done your bird,' Charlie told me.

He was so right.

CHAPTER FIFTEEN

THE SMELLIEST MAN
IN PARKHURST

O n the way to the hotplate one morning, I noticed a pongy prisoner, known as Dirty McSquirty, mooching around the cells. He was going up and down the staircase from landing to landing, looking very intense and still very dirty.

'What's he up to?' I asked Fat Fred as we watched him peering through the cell doors.

'No idea. I just keep well away. Apparently he hasn't washed for five years.'

'Five years? You're havin' a laugh. He hasn't washed since – what – 1977? Bollocks!'

'No, it's true. Look at his face.'

I had a good view of Dirty McSquirty – real name Frank – as we walked past. He looked even filthier than during my previous sightings. He wore a headband and had the appearance of an Apache in those old Wild West films. His face was dark, like a dodgy tan, although that was not the effect of the sunshine during exercise time. It was dirt engrained in the wrinkles in his face.

'He's really niffy today,' Fat Fred said as we slowed down to see what Dirty McSquirty was up to. 'I've never seen him near the showers. He once had a bath and it took us weeks to clean the thing out.'

'Pooh!' I almost choked as I became aware of a heavy, lingering, pungent stench surrounding the unloved and unwanted inmate. 'I see what you mean.'

McSquirty was darting from cell to cell, trying to track down the occupants for a reason still unknown to me. As he moved along the landing I was intrigued by his unnatural-looking black hair. Lumps of shoe polish fell off, giving the game away.

Fred gave me more details: 'He preys on the broken hearted. He finds out who's been dumped by their wife or girlfriend, then moves in big time. He's keen on wedding rings and any sort of gems so he can trade them in for gear. He tells his victims that the rings are only bad memories.'

Later I had a good think to myself and went to find Dirty McSquirty, who was sitting down in a TV room, reading one of the red-top newspapers.

'I'll buy stuff from you,' I suggested, seizing the opportunity for profit.

'Yeah, let's do that,' Frank said, sounding a bit off his head on whatever he was taking.

The scheme worked a treat. I used some of my allowances to buy jewellery from Frank, and then sold the rings and everything to all-comers at a higher price. McSquirty bought his puff, took it back to the heartbroken prisoner's cell, and they both became stoned, making each other more and more miserable.

Frank had saved up to buy an ornate cage for his budgie, Boy Boy. I used to see Boy Boy flying up and down the wing, performing tricks as he went. I joked that he was 'doing his bird' along with the rest of us.

It was bad news for McSquirty when some of the geezers ran out of puff. Where would they get any more from? Frank was sent to see the IRA, who usually had ample supplies. Unfortunately for Frank and Boy Boy, the story took a very sad twist.

When Frank arrived back from his dealings with the IRA, Boy Boy lay there, flat out on the cell bed. He had performed his last trick.

To add insult to injury, the boys made up a story about Boy Boy getting stuck in a door and they had to put him down. They offered their sincere apologies. Really, they had strangled the poor thing.

Even worse for the budgie owner, they said there was a bright side to the tragedy; the cage could be sold for a bit of puff.

Frank could see the logic of this argument. He sold the cage, bought puff for everyone, and that was that. Everything seemed to work out in the end, and Frank continued preying on miserable prisoners without Boy Boy flapping up and down the wing.

'I was tempted to sort out that bloody bird myself,' Charlie said, winking at me as I told him the story of Boy Boy's final moments.

Boy Boy wasn't the only winged inhabitant of the prison system. Prisoners were allowed to keep small birds, and it improved behaviour. It was accepted that some cons would form an emotional bond with their pet. They would read up on how to look after a budgie; men of fifty and over were a common sight in prison libraries throughout the country, finding out about the best bird food, how to clean the cage and all that.

The rules have changed: you can't bring in new feathered birds these days, but old ones can be kept until they die. Sadly, Boy Boy met a premature end. And to Frank's credit, he didn't sing like a canary after his tragic loss.

I occasionally saw Dirty McSquirty walking around with a colossal bloke called Jack. His nickname was 'Bulletproof Jack', because he'd been shot six times by the IRA and survived. He was such a solid-built guy, like a weight-lifter, and that's probably why he had the strength to survive the shootings. Maybe the bullets bounced off him!

Jack's party trick was holding a beer barrel with one hand over his head. McSquirty and Jack were alleged to have been involved on the same bit of work. The story went that they heard a shopkeeper had a fortune hidden under his floorboards. As it happened, there was only a few quid in the shop. They were supposed to have tortured him to get the cash. They were said to have poured petrol in his mouth and then lit it, so he burned from the inside.

Frank always pleaded innocence when he was at Parkhurst. He'd actually worked in the shop and insisted that someone walked in, poured petrol over the shop-keeper and struck a match. Eventually he won an appeal hearing because his conviction wasn't safe.

CHAPTER SIXTEEN
TWO SIDES GOING TO WAR

The power of the Richardson and Kray firms in Parkhurst made a profound impression on me.

Whether Charlie was commenting on Dirty McSquirty or a debate about the parole system on Radio 4, you had to listen. If Reggie asked you to do something, you did it. You were either loyal to one group or the other. It was hard to be 'true to two'. However, I tried my best to treat them with equal respect.

I had become more and more interested in the library and the books on offer. You could go across yourself or write a list in the wing office and they would bring them over to you. There were a couple of librarians and orderlies. The orderlies were prisoners who worked in the library and did lots of running around, delivering books.

Armed robbers, hitmen, murderers, fraudsters and an assortment of other criminals went over and chose books.

The nonces weren't allowed near the place as they would have been killed on the spot.

Charlie didn't go the library; he just read books in his cell. He read all the best books about minerals and passed them on to me with his usual message: 'Expand the mind, expand the mind, Bobby.'

I thought it was quite apt to read *One Flew over the Cuckoo's Nest*, all about rebellion against conformity. Many people at Parkhurst went bonkers and were nutted off to Broadmoor, so I could identify with the book.

I also read factual books, especially about other countries. I appreciated the magic of Asian civilisations, and structures like the Great Wall of China. I found out why structures were built in a certain way and I could see there was a beauty in architecture. It was like an art to me, with the great pyramids and all that. Most of the books I read were academic, like sociology, psychology and law, which were to prove useful for my Open University courses later. It had to be a better than sitting there, watching moron TV.

Reggie wasn't interested in books – he just went down to the gym and belted the punchbag. He kept on talking about trying to secure his future. I was reading books about the law covering house-buying; Reggie saw what I was doing and wanted me to educate one of his young admirers.

'Could you teach one of my boys? It'll help us to know about buying houses for when we get out.'

I sat down with the kid, explained housing law and everything, but it was like talking to a brick wall. The conversation wasn't going anywhere. The kid was bored. He didn't want to know about buying houses. All he wanted was to hang around Reggie and be a gangster.

'Don't waste your time because he's as thick as shit,' Charlie said, and I accepted his advice.

As Reggie and Charlie talked more and more to each other, and seemed reasonably friendly, I joined in on a neutral basis. I had no axe to grind with either firm and I enjoyed the company of both of them. Parkhurst was home to other firms when I was there, but none had a fraction of the influence of the Krays or Richardsons. Their power had to be seen to be believed.

All of a sudden I could feel tension in the air again. Reggie's men were looking serious and keeping themselves to themselves. Charlie's people were also on guard, ready to pounce at the hint of any trouble.

I remembered Charlie saying that Ronnie hated his guts, and wondered if anything was about to kick off. Sure enough, Ronnie did have the hump with Charlie over some old grudge or other.

What happened was this: Ronnie sent one of those 'Now hear this' letters to Reggie, and it said his twin should whack Charlie. That put Reggie in a difficult position because he'd been getting on well with his former opponent. One of the boys on the wing, a young

Jock who scurried around Reggie's cell, whispered the news to me.

'Bobby, I saw the letter to Reggie. It said "fucking do Charlie". It was hard to read, but I could make that bit out. It was in big letters.'

'Leave it with me,' I said, trying not to sound too concerned, although a bloodbath was a possibility. I knew that, with word getting out, both sides would be tooled up, ready to fight to the last man. This was serious.

I sat in my cell and gazed at the stone floor, gathering my thoughts. I was more or less the man in the middle, with no favouritism for either side. This feud had to be stopped before it got any further. Another point to be considered was the fact that some old prisoners were finishing their sentences and wanted to be freed without any aggro. How could I be loyal to two people who might be at each other's throats? I realised that I might be whacked as well. I prepared myself for some tricky negotiations, backwards and forwards across the landing.

'Charlie, could I have a word?'

I walked slowly into Charlie's cell, thinking carefully about what I was about to say. He was sitting at his oversized table, checking stocks and shares in the newspaper. A couple of thick books, all about precious gems, were open. I could see dazzling images of diamonds. Charlie was having a puff and swigging from a mug of tea. I chose my words carefully.

'Charlie, there's something kicking off here and I'm trying to nip it in the bud. Have you set someone up to whack Reggie? I hear Ronnie's upset and I'm wondering if you did anything to annoy him.'

'Nothing at all, Bobby. Reg was in here for a cup of tea yesterday. He seemed okay. He was talking about setting up his mafia operation and asking what I thought. I said it was a load of bollocks, but I don't think he took that in.'

'Nothing else?'

'Na, he was talking about buying houses in the country again. Said they used to own a place down in Hampshire near the sea. He and Ronnie went down at weekends and drank in the Bugle at a place called Hamble. He was very keen on Hamble. He had relatives who fought in various wars and they were treated at a military hospital down south. That's what he was on about.'

'Hold up a minute. I'll be back.'

I jogged along to Reggie's cell. 'Has Ronnie been in touch, saying anything about whacking Charlie?'

I could tell by the expression on Reggie's face that it was true that he had received one of the 'Colonel Biff' letters from his brother. He didn't need to say anything. My worry was that more people were loyal to Charlie, and I couldn't see Reggie surviving any battle in the prison. Reggie's one half of a pair garden shears was unlikely to make any impression.

Back I went to Charlie's cell. 'There is something going on, Charlie, since you had your chat with Reggie. I think we need to sort it out now.'

'I'm not afraid of Reggie Kray, understand? If he wants to go down to the gym we can sort it out. I'll give him a straightener. That'll shut him up.'

Charlie's offer of a straightener, or a good solid punch, could have made things worse, but I relayed the information anyway. Reggie, I was sure, could still handle himself in a fight and might even surprise Charlie.

'Look, Reggie,' I said. 'You've got your steaks coming in, you've got film stars visiting you and the screws leave you alone. You don't want any trouble. If it kicks off in here, there will be no more of all that. You'll get extra bird on top, so will Charlie, lots of people will get hurt and it'll end in disaster. What about if we put the lid on it and sort anything out when you're all released?'

'Okay,' Reggie answered. 'See what Charlie says.'

Back I went to Charlie: 'What do you think about the plan?'

'Yeah, sort it when we get out.'

I stepped out of Charlie's cell, onto the landing, and spotted the young Jock who'd tipped me off. He made a sign with his thumb, asking if it was thumbs-up or down.

I put my thumb in the air, and he ran over to me with a small bottle of whisky.

'All in a day's work,' I told him. 'Thanks for the tip. A few people would have been killed, that's for sure.'

The Jock probably didn't realise the full extent of what could have happened, but his quick thinking saved several lives. We had just prevented all-out war at Parkhurst.

CHAPTER SEVENTEEN

AND THEN THERE WAS FRANKIE FRASER

Frankie Fraser was still on the move, being sent to high security jails all over the country.

Shortly after the truce was agreed between the Krays and the Richardsons, I spotted Frankie himself walking along the landing at Parkhurst. I hoped that this would be an extended stay!

Like any other new arrival, he was carrying one of his boxes of possessions. Someone like Frankie was a face to people who were in for fraud or lesser crimes. He was a legend and demanded respect at all times.

His life of crime began about ten years before I was born, when he was sent to borstal for breaking into a hosiery store. Those were tough times, with no employment and no money in a slum area. People had to steal to survive.

Frankie made regular appearances at Durham, Leicester, Gloucester and many more prisons. He must have been to them all.

Charlie Richardson had told me all about the riots of '69, and Frankie's role. I had met Frankie before and saw him again when he had a brief stay at Parkhurst shortly after I arrived. Now here I was, face-to-face with the Richardsons' enforcer once more on the landing of 'B' wing.

Frankie's cell was a few doors away from me on the opposite side, close to the screws' office. He was well dressed when I saw him, with grey flannels, a blue shirt and black jacket.

Frankie wore slippers. The reason, he said, was that they didn't let him wear shoes when he was in punishment cells on bread and water. When punishment finished and he could put his shoes on again, he refused to wear them as a matter of principle. Once, he took aim and actually hit a governor on the head with a well-directed slipper. It was a friendly approach, considering that I had put a blade against a governor's head!

I was wearing pressed trousers and shirt, with newly polished shoes, so we both looked smart as we stood chatting on the landing of 'B' wing. He would have been nearly sixty years old, with me just over half his age early in 1983. He was in pretty good shape, and certainly didn't look sixty.

'You're still here then,' Frankie said as his dark, dark eyes looked me up and down. 'I might only be here for a few days. They're trying to break me and make things as difficult as they can. They'll never win.'

'It's hard to believe that you're here along with Charlie Richardson and Reggie Kray,' I said, meaning every word.

Reggie and Ronnie had wanted Frankie to work for them, but instead he chose to work as a hard, hard man for the Richardsons. When he joined their manor, Frank said his new employers were miles ahead of the Krays in brain power and everything else that mattered. Others in the business were heard to say that, when Frankie joined the Richardsons, it was like China getting the atomic bomb.

Now they were all banged up in the same place; but if there were old scores to settle, Frankie didn't mention any. In fact, as we stood outside Frankie's cell, chatting, Charlie Richardson walked past, then Reggie and his young boys, and they all waved! I could see that Frankie had as much respect for Reggie and Ronnie as he had for Charlie Richardson.

'I knew Ron and Reg before I knew Charlie Richardson and his brother Eddie. We go back a long time. The twins brought my sister to prison – wherever I was – for visiting.'

Frankie got seven years for cutting another gangster, Jack Spot. He was part of a group who attacked Jack Spot in the street back in 1956. His real name was Jack Comer, but he said he was always 'on the spot' when Jews were being sorted out. Another version was that he got the name from a large black mole on his left cheek.

The attack was carried out on the orders of Billy Hill, a rival gangster. Hill and Spot had worked together, and were two of the original main men in the London crime scene. Their activities inspired the Krays and the Richardsons. But when they fell out, Hill was quick to mutilate his ex-partner in crime, with Frankie playing the lead role. Then again, that was his style.

In his early years he was certified insane a couple of times, earning the nickname 'Mad' Frankie Fraser. He didn't appear mad to me. When he was in Broadmoor, Frankie stayed out of trouble to avoid being heavily sedated.

'There are a few IRA in here,' I told Frankie. 'Well, they come and go. There was even an IRA man at Kingston when I went there. I've never had any trouble with them. They back up anyone who's complaining about the screws.'

'I believe I'm an honorary member of the IRA,' Frankie grinned.

'Hold up a minute, an honorary member? They are staunch and will support you, I'll say that for them.'

Frankie gave me more details. 'A few years ago I attacked a group of prison officers in Bristol. There were three of them and I really got stuck in. It had to go before magistrates as usual and three IRA people gave evidence to support my case. That was because I supported them during the riots here – in Parkhurst.'

'Charlie filled me in on the riots, Frank. It was all over the papers. I was getting done for a sawn-off shotgun around then. I was only fifteen or sixteen.'

Frankie Fraser was highly intelligent, articulate and very funny. He told me his mother and father let him down because they were straightgoers. Also, that his sister Eva was a brilliant shoplifter, but then she married and stopped thieving. Frankie never forgave her because he had to buy all his own shirts.

'I always wished I'd been on the Great Train Robbery,' he told me with a familiar twinkle in his eyes. 'It was a brilliant operation. I couldn't join in, though, because I was on the run. I was asked to go on the job by Tommy Wisbey. He was a bookie and one of the robbers. The police were after me, so I could have embarrassed everyone. I had to say I couldn't take part, and it was one of my biggest ever regrets.'

Frankie was quite happy to tell me about his incredible life. I enjoyed hearing it from the horse's mouth and encouraged him to continue. He even told me that he received eighteen strokes of the cat-o'-nine-tails for assaulting the governor at Shrewsbury prison. That was at the end of the Second World War, when he would have been around twenty-one.

He admitted to much more serious misdemeanours. As far back as 1951, Frankie tried to hang the governor of Wandsworth prison. Frank, a free man for once, was upset at previous punishments and waited for his victim on Wandsworth Common. Frank strung him up on a tree with his dog. The governor survived because the branch bent down, although the dog died.

Frankie kept chatting: 'You know Charlie's brother, Eddie, was jailed for five years, like me, after all the fighting at Mr Smith's club. Eddie got ten years, same as me, when we were all up for the torture. I didn't use the pliers, but I wish now I had.

'Actually, Eddie and I had a great scheme going with fruit machines in the early days. We were putting them in all over the place. They would always make a profit, because that's what they were designed to do. We could even give the clubs 40 per cent of the takings. I made sure that the clubs took our machines and no one else's. Lovely, it was. Lovely.'

Through the grapevine I had heard about a fracas in the place where the fruit machines were stored, and it all started in a famous club that was frequented by gangsters and celebrities. Frankie told me the story.

'A fight broke out at the Astor Club in Mayfair – that's where we all used to go in the sixties. I just left quietly, not wanting to get involved, but when I was waiting outside for my driver, Eric Mason appeared and said he would tell Reggie and Ronnie.'

'Tell them what?' I asked, knowing that Mason was a feared, well-built figure who could handle himself with his fists.

'Tell them that I caused the fight.'

Frankie said that was unacceptable as he hadn't started anything, so he decided to take action.

'I threw Mason in the car and took him to the place where we kept our fruit machines. I hit him with an axe

I'd got from Harrods. He was trying to protect himself, but the axe went through his hands and nailed his fingers to his head.'

'How did he survive that?' I wondered.

'Well, we put him back in the car and threw him outside the Royal London Hospital so they must have patched him up. I was more worried about the axe. Lovely axe, it was.'

That was Frankie's version, so why shouldn't I believe him? I'd heard Eric Mason's version. He claimed he had been sitting with a large group in the Astor Club. Mason said Frankie was with the Richardsons, some Scottish gangsters and a few others, and Frankie stabbed one of the rival group.

In the melee that followed, Eric said he was taken in a car to Tottenham Court Road and a cellar where the one-armed bandits were kept. He said he put his hand over his head to ward off a blow, and the axe went through his fingers. Both men agreed with the final result; Eric's hands were pinned to his head with an axe.

Time to lighten the mood, I thought. Frankie was well-known for his support of Arsenal. At that time, in the early eighties, they had the likes of David O'Leary and Kenny Sansom in defence, while Pat Jennings stood in goal with his enormous pair of hands.

'Third in the league this year so we qualify for the UEFA Cup,' Frankie told me proudly. 'I'd rather be at Highbury watching a game than stewing in here.'

'I can't offer the same standard from Parkhurst FC,' I said. 'But they do play some sort of football. Let's have a look.'

We went down the staircase, into the compound and down a hill towards a tarmac football pitch beside a basketball court. The area for football was much smaller than a normal pitch, yet there were so many players of all shapes and sizes. It could have been fifteen-a-side.

Both teams had at least seven forwards. No referee would have wanted to enter the fray in the middle of that mob.

'Look, they're all offside,' Frankie laughed. 'I like their tactics. We should get twenty goals. Lovely.'

The offside rule, or any rule, could never be applied with groups of players standing on the opposing goal lines. It was a 'kick and rush' arrangement. The goalkeeper kicked the ball up in the air and a dozen or so players raced after it, feet flying in all directions. Their target was more like a toy beach ball that you would find in a novelty shop, rather than a football.

As for the game, it was just a mish-mash. Some of the team wore shorts and T-shirts, while others had on their work overalls and boots. You couldn't tell who was on either side because of the many different colours on show.

We could see why the players were running around on the tarmac. Frankie and I walked along past a collection of workshops and came across another football area on a pitch with no grass. For some reason there was a trench in the middle of the pitch. The touchlines were tight to the playing area, leaving no room for manoeuvre and a danger to life and limb for a flying winger.

'I think you're safer when you're doing your enforcing,' I told Frankie. 'This looks like a danger zone!'

We both had a good laugh, trudged back to our cells and prepared for the evening ahead, with our meals and TV to look forward to.

One thing became clear: Frankie was not afraid of anyone or anything. But he was always there for the prisoners. If anyone complained about a screw, he was at their side. If a rat had to be dealt with, Frankie was there to sort it out. If a spokesman was needed to highlight an issue such as poor food, Frankie stepped up to the plate. His word was his bond. If he said he was going to do something, he would do it without hesitation.

People talk about notorious people like Charles Bronson, but they weren't in the same league as Frankie Fraser. He was the most subversive man in the country and, when he was active, the most dangerous.

Did he pull out teeth with pliers during the Charlie Richardson mock trials? I don't think so. His savage right handers knocked enough teeth out without the need for pliers.

There will never be another Frankie Fraser.

CHAPTER EIGHTEEN

GADDAFI'S HITMAN AND THE BOXER

'Have a look at this book. Everyone should read it. This is the perfect book. *The Green Book*. It has been written by our great leader, Colonel Muammar Gaddafi.'

It was green all right, but looked more like a pamphlet. There was Arabic writing on the front so I had no idea what was going on. I could see it was a slim volume, to say the least. I reckoned it was Gaddafi's way of explaining his ideology – just as the *Little Red Book* explained the thinking of Chairman Mao Tse-tung.

'I will translate for you.'

The imposing figure of Ben Hassan Muhammad El Masri – Colonel Gaddafi's hitman in the UK – stood outside my cell. We were both hitmen, although my targets had been rats in firms, rather than political opponents.

'I keep seeing you in Charlie's cell. I thought it would be better to have a good chat. I know all about your armed robberies. I believe that you will want to know all about my book.'

Hassan, as we called him, was an executioner who whacked opponents of the Libyan regime. The People's Bureau had ordered the killing of dissident Muhammad Ramadan outside Regent's Park Mosque in the spring of 1980. Now, exactly three years later, in the summer of 1983, he was still praising his great leader to the hilt.

Hassan had an accomplice, Nagib Mufta Gasmi. Both were arrested near the mosque and later convicted. They were jailed for life.

Those were brutal times in London. Another Libyan assassin, known as Al Gidal, murdered a Libyan lawyer who was known to be a dissident. Al Gidal was an associate of Hassan and Gasmi. He was jailed for life, too. Hassan ended up at Parkhurst, but I had no idea what happened to his mates.

I met Hassan shortly before the murder of WPC Yvonne Fletcher outside what was then the Libyan embassy in St James's Square. Automatic gunfire mowed down anti-Gaddafi protesters. Yvonne, unarmed, was shot in the stomach and died shortly afterwards. Her fiancé was by her side as she lay on the street, dying. The gunfire came from inside the embassy.

Several years later, Gaddafi's government accepted responsibility for her death and paid compensation to the family.

I looked Hassan up and down as he stood there, towering above me. Hassan was a good six-and-a-half feet, as I'd noticed when I first met him in Charlie Richardson's cell. He was so distinctive with his black, curly hair, jet-black eyes and little moustache.

He flicked open *The Green Book*. 'This is the solution for the problem of democracy.'

Hassan told me that the world needed to be rescued from the failures of Western democracy and communism. There should be no elections or political parties, and the people must learn to rule themselves. At least I think that's what he was saying.

'How can you have someone winning an election and most of the people who voted don't agree with the policies? Your system makes no sense.'

'I'll check out your little book when I join the Open University,' I joked.

'Come and have a cup of tea,' Hassan offered, pointing to his cell.

I walked with him to the cell, next to Charlie Richardson. Charlie waved as we walked past, giving me a wink because he knew what was in store.

As Hassan's cell door opened, I rubbed my eyes with disbelief. It was like opening the door to the room of a four-star hotel. There were all sorts of furnishings, coffee tables and rugs – plus a set of purple velvet curtains! I noticed that he also had a top-notch Roberts radio. There was even a posh leather armchair. A butler, probably a paid prisoner, glided along the landing with a tray after making deliveries to the luxurious cell. The bloke was even done up like a butler. You couldn't make it up, I know.

'There is a difference between us,' Hassan told me sternly. 'You and your London armed robbers are criminals. I am not a criminal.'

I was flabbergasted: 'Hold up a minute. You whacked that bloke outside the mosque. That sounds like murder in anyone's book.'

'It was a legitimate execution on the orders of my leader. I do not feel any guilt, as I am a political prisoner. If your government told you to execute an enemy of the state in another country, then you would do it, but it doesn't mean you are a criminal. Look at your IRA. They say they are political prisoners, fighting for a cause. It is the same with me, following orders in the interests of my country.'

'Well, you're in here with the rest of us. It doesn't matter if you shot him, poisoned him, tortured him, executed him or pushed the geezer off a cliff. The Old Bill won't see any difference. The judge didn't see any difference!'

'We will have to agree to disagree, as you say. What's the worst thing you did then, Bobby? If you are an armed robber you must have shot people. You must have terrified people.'

It was an opportunity to educate Hassan about the weapon that provided my livelihood.

'Well, I've done a lot of horrible things. We did have a shotgun we called Kennedy. It was what we called a sawn-off, and looked like a pirate's pistol. People lived in fear of it. The thing caused terror, although in our world it was a way of keeping order in the manor. A manor was our territory. These weren't jobs for the Old Bill. The police, I mean. The only way to keep things sweet was to use violence. Sometimes Kennedy became the "Stinger".'

Hassan screwed up his face. 'Bobby, I have used all sorts of weapons. I trained with automatics, semi-automatics and pistols. But I never heard of a Stinger.'

'Well, what happened was, we had some trouble in the manor. We adapted Kennedy for special bits of work.'

'Special bits of work?'

'A bit of work is going on a job or some business. That's how it is in our world. Well, a couple of Turkish brothers were harassing a Greek Cypriot family. They got their daughter on drugs. They needed to be chucked off the manor as soon as possible.'

'What did you do with Kennedy?'

'I loaded one cartridge with buckshot and the other with hard rock salt. The brothers had a small garage, so a couple of us went there with the Stinger and laid it on the line to them. One of the brothers was working under a car. The gun was aimed at his legs. It went off, blasting him with the rock salt. He didn't know if I was pellets, bullets or whatever. He was just screaming with pain.'

'This is very intimidating,' Hassan, said, sounding shocked. 'What happened next?'

We aimed Kennedy against the other brother's head. We could almost smell his fear. We said they had twenty-four hours to leave the manor. They were gone, lively, in well under that time.'

'Why rock salt?'

'It all melted into the wounds. They say it's the worst pain ever. Well, it's probably as sore as when a blade is run through garlic, then pierces the skin and everything puffs up. There was no trace for the forensics, with the salt, after it all healed. People would never go to the Old Bill, anyway, with the drug dealing going on.'

Hassan was unrepentant. 'Our shootings were totally different. We have a great country and a great leader. I was only doing my duty. A death warrant had been issued. I did not commit a murder. It was an execution, authorised by our leader. I shot to kill, and not with salt.'

'Yeah, well, let's leave it there,' I suggested, still sizing up this unusual character.

Hassan was a devout Muslim. I'd seen him doing the prayers when he arrived. I could tell that he was well looked after from the outside. An imam arranged for the finest food to be brought in and, from the remains of the meal he'd just eaten, I observed it was a few leagues above our eggs and chips.

I sat down on his leather upholstered visitor's chair while he stood, admiring the contents of *The Green Book.*

He was still receiving his wages, judging by the paper-work on a side table.

I munched on an exotic sweet while he chatted about his country, politics in the USA, politics in Britain and the amount of oil in the Middle East. He knew so much about minerals, which meant many in-depth chats with Charlie Richardson. Hassan was highly educated. He rose to the rank of general in the Libyan Army and served as an intelligence officer. This was no moron with a gun.

In his short time with us, he had shared his goodies around the wing. They were welcomed by everyone. Whatever he had, he was happy to dish out and he made a lot of friends that way.

'I am looking forward to going home,' Hassan said firmly.

'They call you a terrorist,' I replied. 'They'll never let you out. They don't give in to terrorists. I'm not saying you're a terrorist, but that's how they see you.'

His black, black eyes stared at me. 'Bobby, believe me, soon I will be gone. I won't serve that sentence. But I will keep in touch with my friends here.'

I wished Hassan all the best, thanked him for his hospitality, and headed back to my cell. I looked back and saw that he was preparing for one of his fitness sessions. Hassan was fit and toned. He spent as much time as he could running around the exercise yard.

'Gaddafi's book has a couple of fair points,' Charlie chirped as I strolled past his cell.

'Oh? It's all about politics and democracy, isn't it?'

Charlie had read *The Green Book* from cover to cover: 'The kitchen here could take some tips from him.'

'Tips from Gaddafi?'

'He campaigns against mechanised poultry farms, saying the meat of wild birds is more tasty and nourishing because they grow naturally. Also, they're fed naturally, I remember the book said.'

'So the kitchen should serve up wild birds ... '

'They could serve up cats that would taste better than the chicken in here,' Charlie laughed.

'There are none left. Nagi ate them all.'

Charlie and I both burst out laughing. He remembered at once how I had supplied a prisoner called Nagi with meat, assumed to be rabbit. I bought the animals from a working party in the grounds. However, the scammers skinned the beasts before delivery and it turned out that, over a considerable period, Nagi had eaten all of the prison cats.

Charlie recalled more about the unfortunate incident. 'Everyone went "meow, meow" whenever he ventured out of his cell – and whenever he wasn't violently ill because of the thought of eating the cats.'

I opened my cell door, switched on the radio and settled down to Radio 4. Charlie kept on and on at me to improve my education, and Radio 4 was still the best choice on the airwaves. It was *Book at Bedtime* again for me.

As I lay there on my iron bed, I reflected on Hassan's beliefs. He was a gentleman. He was generous. He was highly intelligent and well educated. And yet he would blow away an opponent of Gaddafi's regime without a second thought.

Bill the Bomb, a new arrival, was a professional boxer. He was mean, tough and took no prisoners. He looked like a gorilla, walked like a gorilla and snarled – probably like a gorilla would snarl.

I kept encountering these people as they came and went within the prison system. Bill the Bomb – real name Billy Williams – was something I had never seen before. He was a violent, rough-and-tough fighting machine. At any time of day, he looked as if he might lash out.

Now, Bill the Bomb could have gone far with his boxing. He boasted that he was taken to America by promoter Angelo Dundee, who worked with sixteen world champions. He even claimed that he sparred with Muhammad Ali, one of the greatest sporting figures of the twentieth century.

According to Bill the Bomb, Angelo reckoned that he could have been a world champion. However, Bill got mixed up with white powder and a mafia wife. He had to come back to England, lively, or they would have rubbed him out. So that was the end of his professional boxing career.

I'd heard all of this on the outside, while I was drinking in the pubs and clubs. I'd also read in the papers that he held someone down while an accomplice in a car ran over the unfortunate victim. His long list of violent incidents and driving offences brought him to Parkhurst.

The former boxer had a pub on Barking Road. Loads of Irish road diggers, fifteen- or twenty-handed, went inside and complained when the Guinness ran out. Bill and his mate waded into them and flattened them all. There used to be a horse in there, drinking beer from a pint glass. Bill also had a reputation for locking publicans in their premises and taking over the businesses. He was a man to be feared on many levels.

Bill the Bomb appeared at Parkhurst on the landing above me, on the threes. They must have realised that he wasn't a potential escaper, unlikely to hack away at the roof, so they put him on the top floor. He was just violent and wanted to hurt as many people as possible with his huge fists. They were as big as the hands of Frankie Fraser's football hero, Arsenal goalkeeper Pat Jennings.

'I've never met you but I've heard all about you,' I said truthfully.

'Same here', Bill the Bomb answered, shaking hands.

He looked like a real thug – a real animal. He was about five-foot-ten, with bulging muscles and an aggressive stance. He was in his thirties, starting to go slightly grey, and just looked intimidating. He was keen to know about my dark past.

'Did you make much money working as a gangster?' Bill the Bomb asked, touching a nerve.

'I've never been a gangster, just a businessman,' I said, sounding as calm as I could under the circumstances.

'Oh, you're not a gangster then,' he apologised.

'The most famous story about me is 100 per cent true. Kennedy was the name for my sawn-off shotgun. He had a brother. It was a Smith & Wesson .38 revolver. A guy called Johnny told my girlfriend she was going out with a gangster. I've always referred to myself as a businessman, making a living from a life of crime. I wasn't a loud gangster, mouthing off in pubs, causing rucks.'

'Okay, I can see that,' Bill the Bomb nodded.

'I knew Johnny drank in the Hercules pub in Holloway Road. There he was, making a lot of noise at the bar, covered in gold bracelets and everything like that. I asked him to come outside on the pretext that I had some work for him. We went down an alley and I produced Kennedy's brother. I stuck the barrel in his mouth. I said to Johnny, "I am not a gangster. I'm a businessman trying hard to earn a crust – understood?" He seemed to understand and he was shaking all over.'

Bill the Bomb was getting the picture: 'You didn't shoot him, then?'

'I took the barrel out of his mouth and smashed him in the face with the butt. He understood all right.'

Well, Bill the Bomb was in there for violence and so the screws should have known to stay well clear of him. I had no reason to avoid Bill; this was a new face, and a chatty one at that.

'One of them wants to take me on,' Bill the Bomb told me over breakfast, the morning after he arrived. 'The screw heard I'm a boxer and wants to do it fair and square in the gym. I told him that, if I hit him, I'd get nicked for it. The screw said I wouldn't get nicked, so it's happening. I'm sure the screw is a straightgoer.'

I gaped at Bill the Bomb's muscles and feared for the screw's safety. He pointed out the screw and, to be fair, this was an athletic muscular type who could no doubt pack a decent punch. All the screw knew was that Bill the Bomb had done some boxing. He had no idea what to expect.

In the afternoon, then, they shaped up to each other in the gym with their gloves at the ready. I could see what was coming as I peeked round the door. The screw, called Jamie, was jumping up and down, shadow boxing, and looking the real deal.

Jamie gave a gentle jab or two. Bill the Bomb stood there, like a dangerous animal, staring at him. The screw gave another gentle jab and lined up a punch. It looked a good enough effort, except that Bill ducked and the punch missed. I could see that my new friend was taking the piss.

Jamie did some ducking and diving, jabbing now and again and throwing the odd punch. The only one that landed was a mild body punch that made Bill smile. He was really taking the piss now.

The screw seemed to be growing in confidence, because Bill the Bomb was just standing there. Some more jabs from the screw; this time his fearsome opponent brushed them away as if he was flicking a fly off his arm.

All of a sudden Bill decided he had been taking the mickey for too long. He shuffled and delivered a couple of powerful jabs with his left hand. The screw leaned back, surprised, but came in for more, not realising that Bill the Bomb was a lethal fighting machine.

Crunch. The whole room shook as Bill delivered a fierce uppercut with his right hand, knocking the screw's head back, almost off his shoulders. With that, Bill sat down on the floor and guzzled a can of drink as he watched the screw lying flat out.

Slowly but surely, the screw came to his senses and began to lift himself from the floor. He looked unsteady, and I could see a large lump appearing above his eye. He realised that Bill, in a different, more evil mood, could have killed him.

'I've never seen a punch like that, close up,' I confessed to Bill as he sipped his drink.

'I held back at first, but I was thirsty so I finished him off.'

By this time Jamie had recovered enough to open a can of his own drink. He slurped it down quickly. To be fair to the screw, he nodded to Bill, appreciating that he had been pulverised.

The dejected screw left the room to resume his duties and no doubt explain how he had fallen and hit his head. I never saw him in his boxing gear again.

A couple of days later, Bill the Bomb came along the landing, shadow boxing as he went. He punched imaginary targets, swinging just as hard as when he floored Jamie the screw in the gym. He seemed to be hanging around, waiting for me to appear.

'Good morning, Bill, everything okay?' I asked politely as he jabbed at the cell door.

'I'm all right, but your mate has vanished.'

'Eh?'

'Well, the geezer you were chatting to. The one you call the assassin. Hassan or something. He's still got those big curtains, but everything else seems to have gone. It looks a bit bare in there. Last time I looked, he had some fancy cups and all sorts of plates.'

'Mail,' a loud voice echoed along the landing as I pondered over Hassan's disappearance. 'Give this to Charlie for me. He's gone walkabout.'

John, the tubby screw who looked like Captain Birdseye, was approaching with a sack of mail and holding up a postcard. He handed it over with a smile, a nod and his usual 'bad weather on the Solent' update. He said it was 'blowin' a hooley' again.

I left Bill the Bomb to his shadow boxing and had a look at the postcard as I walked along towards Hassan's cell. The card had an exotic scene, showing Tripoli. I remembered that Hassan always said he would be freed; I assumed he'd been exchanged for someone held by the Libyans.

The postcard read: 'Dear Charlie. Please pass on my best wishes to everyone. I hope Bobby, Gary and Reggie are okay. I am here with my family, and life is good. I am going to still keep fit with my running. Keep reading *The Green Book*. Your people will learn a lot from it. I might not be able to keep in touch again. Please tell Nez that I am sorry I could not eat his pork with the bits of Muriel, and I could not share your hooch drink. Your loyal friend, Hassan.'

Despite that stern exterior, Hassan had a sense of humour, after all!

'Told you he had gone,' Bill the Bomb said in a 'told you so' tone as he caught up with me and peered over my shoulder. 'Maybe he's gone out to shoot more of those Libyans. He's an executioner, that geezer.'

Bill's impression of the cell was correct. The purple velvet curtains still hung there, shielding nothing apart from a couple of bare tables and a bed, stripped of its expensive covers. I was hoping that perhaps he'd left his radio, but that was gone as well. I thought briefly about flogging the curtains. I decided to leave them, assuming that his people would arrive to collect them.

I shrugged my shoulders and returned to my cell for a spot of reading. *The Green Book* wasn't on my reading list, although I did miss my pal and wondered what he was up to.

We never heard any more from Ben Hassan Muhammad El Masri, the gentleman killer.

CHAPTER NINETEEN
THE MOST EVIL MAN IN PARKHURST

'There he is, look!'

Charlie Richardson, having a walk with me around the exercise yard, pointed to a prisoner, handcuffed to two screws, being led to the Vulnerable Prisoners Unit. Perhaps he'd been taken to the hospital or to 'C' wing to check if he was mad.

This furtive character, glancing round all the time, had a thin, long face, dark hair that came forward in a 'V', thin, cruel lips and staring eyes. His nose had a bit of a point on it. Those eyes were really scary. A swirling wind whipped up on that day in October 1983, blowing leaves around the nervous inmate and his guards.

'Be careful if you have a cup of tea with him,' Charlie Richardson warned, as a twinkle appeared in his steely blue eyes. 'That's Graham Young.'

'I've heard people talk about him since I arrived here. That's the first sighting, though. He poisoned his mother, didn't he?'

'Stepmum. He slipped her regular doses of his favourite poisons and watched her die. He enjoyed it. The doctors thought she had a virus or something. Young's real mum died shortly after his birth, and he grew up to hate his stepmother. Molly, she was called.'

'I get the picture. He's mad, then.'

Charlie nodded and passed me a newspaper, with a headline saying 'Teacup Poisoner'.

'Some people didn't survive after their cup of tea,' Charlie announced, still with that twinkle in his eyes.

'Maybe he wants to do some of us?'

'He hasn't whacked anyone in here, so I'm sure we'll be okay.'

'Should we be tooled up?'

Charlie was full of mischief. 'It wouldn't make any difference.'

'Should I be on guard for a right hander?'

'He's not violent.'

'But he makes up potions and all that game.'

'He can even kill with the moss from the windowsill, as you'll have heard before,' Charlie beamed.

'He must be mad.'

Charlie knew the case backwards. 'Yes, he is. But we're safe. He's over there in a special unit with the Ripper, the Black Panther and all that lot.'

I was really intrigued. I read that article in the news-paper, which jogged my memory about Graham Young. His barbaric methods stunned the country in the sixties and seventies.

He even kept diaries on how various poisons affected people.

His hero was the infamous Dr Crippen who poisoned and dismembered his wife. As a schoolboy, Young was also fascinated by Adolf Hitter, wearing swastikas at every opportunity. He said that Hitler was misunder-stood. To add to his weird personality, Young read all about the occult and tried to get other children involved. It's believed that he sacrificed cats. The local cat popula-tion decreased when Young was around, and his bizarre activities could provide the explanation.

Young was mesmerised by poisons and the way they could cause a slow, lingering death. He learned all about chemicals at an early age and decided to try them out on his family.

'He received a chemistry set as a present,' Charlie said. 'After that, he started to poison his school pals and family. One pal in his science class became ill after Graham sneaked rat poison or something into his drink. They went for a trip to the zoo and Graham gave him some lemonade to make him better. It only made him worse because the lemonade contained more poison.'

'I can't believe he poisoned his family,' I said, amazed at Young's antics.

'He would poison the Sunday joint and make sure he didn't eat the dodgy bit.'

Charlie explained that Young managed to get hold of the lethal ingredients, and then administered doses over long periods to check the effects. He watched, taking in every detail, as his victims writhed in agony.

Anybody at Parkhurst who wanted to get 'out of their nut' would ask Young – if they could get access to him – for his secret recipes. He had a reputation for dreaming up all sorts of concoctions. I would have been worried about the addition of poisons!

Lennie the Lid had some more details about Young: 'He could make a drug like LSD from crispbread. He would wrap some in wet tissue, crush it all up and leave it for three weeks. What happens is that a natural spore grows on the rye and it has the same effect as acid. It blows your mind.'

I read more about Young in the prison library. That pal in the science class, Christopher Williams, had really suffered. The only positive thing from the boy's point of view was that Young couldn't monitor the effects of the poisons in a home situation.

That was why he experimented on his family: he could check on the effects and keep a meticulous diary. It was early in 1961 that his nearest and dearest began to show symptoms – and Young's father even suspected his son at one stage. But the dad thought it was more likely that the boy had been careless, spilling a chemical from his chemistry set or something like that.

No one imagined that Young would have deliberately poisoned his own family. He was ill himself sometimes; that could have been deliberate to keep him in the clear, or careless use of his poisons.

Young's father suspected him once again. The boy's sister, Winifred, was poisoned late in 1961 but no action was taken. The sneaky poisoner had slipped something nasty into her tea, but she was taken to hospital and recovered. Graham concocted a story about his sister using family teacups when she shampooed her hair. How do you prove a deliberate act of poisoning, especially if the victims just seem to have some sort of virus?

Young concentrated on his stepmother. He never got on with Molly and decided to administer regular doses of his concoctions. She writhed in agony in the back garden while Young looked on, assessing her symptoms and recording every tiny detail of her suffering. Doctors were baffled as her condition grew worse and she died in excruciating pain.

Her death was put down to other causes – not poisoning – and Young suggested, successfully, that she should be cremated, burning all of the evidence. It appears that Molly developed a tolerance to antimony and so he gave her a dose of thallium. At the funeral, several people began vomiting. Yes, at the funeral.

Well, after Molly passed away in agony, father Fred displayed symptoms of vomiting and cramping. He was diagnosed with antimony poisoning. Still, Fred didn't report his son – but the school chemistry teacher contacted the Old Bill after finding poisons and information about notorious poisoners in the boy's desk. The game was up.

At this stage, Young was only fourteen years old. He admitted poisoning his father, sister and school pal. Of course, he couldn't be held responsible for the death of his stepmother because of the cremation. He was sent to Broadmoor for a minimum of fifteen years.

At Broadmoor the experiments continued. An inmate, John Berridge, died from cyanide poisoning. Was Young responsible? The death was recorded as suicide. Staff and inmates were at risk from the tea urn, which mysteriously contained ingredients such as sugar soap, used by decorators.

Now this I found hard to understand: the doctors thought he had been cured and said he should be released. Young even told a psychiatric nurse that he would kill someone for every year he'd been in Broadmoor, but no one believed him and the release was arranged.

And so the Teacup Poisoner, eager to kill again, was allowed out early in 1971 at the age of twenty-three. He stayed in a hostel, enjoying some contact with wary family members. He stocked up on the various poisons required for his experiments. Two people there became ill. One was in so much pain that he took his own life.

The rejuvenated poisoner became a storeman at a photographic supply company where materials like thallium were used. These simply added to supplies obtained from pharmacists who had no idea of Young's intentions.

In the workplace, Young was always keen to make the tea and coffee. His boss, Bob Egle, developed cramps and dizziness. Bob, who was fifty-nine, was thought to have a bug going around at the time. He recovered at home, but became ill when he returned to his job: the evil work of the Teacup Poisoner. He died in agony in hospital, to Young's delight. The killer was even happier that the death was put down as pneumonia.

The situation in the workplace became desperate. Everyone was off sick, suffering from cramps, loss of hair, sexual problems and various illnesses. The photographic company thought that perhaps chemicals were leaking somewhere in the building or that water was contaminated. Another worker, Fred Biggs, who was sixty, died a painful death. He took too long to pass away, according to the record in Young's diary.

When seventy workers developed symptoms, Young brazenly suggested that thallium from the photographic process might be to blame. The doctor who visited was suspicious when Young displayed impeccable knowledge of chemicals. He contacted the Old Bill.

Young denied everything and the case went to trial. However, the evidence was overwhelming. The diary entries condemned him, and he received four life sentences.

The jury wasn't allowed to know about his previous misdemeanours, yet still found him guilty and he was sent to Parkhurst.

After the case there was a review of the handling of prisoners who were mentally unstable.

I found out that the Parkhurst vicar invited all the weirdos, including the Yorkshire Ripper, to Bible readings and afternoon tea. Anyone who was sane never went. But the vicar refused to invite the Teacup Poisoner for obvious reasons.

Graham Young sounded more dangerous than all of the killers in Parkhurst put together. I was glad not to see him patrolling our landing with a set of test tubes and packages of lethal poisons.

Although he was in the next building, I thought he could probably use cleaning fluid and all that to make some horrible lethal poison, then slip it into our food or drink. The whole idea of Young being anywhere in prison gave screws and cons the creeps.

'Cor, that's horrific, poisoning your own family,' Reggie Kray used to say.

Reggie loved family life. He liked mums, dads, old girls and looking after elderly people.

Charlie was more into the psychology of it all. He liked nothing better than studying the weirdos during what he called loon nights. He wished he could have heard Young's story, first hand.

Charlie told me: 'People write books about these lunatics. But they're in here, so we can study them ourselves. The only thing you can say about Young is that he is totally bonkers.'

Charlie was right, but he also recognised that there was a fag paper between a maniac and a genius. I was glad that we weren't allowed to mix with Young. He could never be trusted. He could slip something into your tea or onto a biscuit, relishing the results of his actions. If you went to the loo, he was capable of putting something on the toilet paper. That's why he had to be kept away from the rest. He enjoyed the opportunity of observing a long, drawn-out and agonising death.

His brilliance, if you could call it that, didn't go unnoticed. I remember hearing that drugs companies contacted Young because of his skill with chemicals. He wrote to them, suggesting particular ingredients for lip gloss and perfumes. Really, he was a genius. However, I doubt if the companies sent a rep to see him because of the risk of death.

Young saw everyone as a lab rat, not as a human being. The authorities made a huge balls-up, letting him out to kill again, and I don't think anyone took responsibility. He was a psychopath, but what happens is that the people assessing these maniacs can be nutters as well. They become so involved with the loonies. It's a contagious thing. I've always found that most psychiatrists you meet are a bit weird, anyway.

People talk about the Krays, the Richardsons and the IRA. Yes, they were violent people, but never as dangerous as Graham Young.

Young was one of life's anomalies. The Ripper did what he did because of whatever religious belief he had. Ian Brady carried out his crimes for sexual masochistic pleasure or whatever. But Young wasn't a human being – he was like a Dr Frankenstein.

We had many debates. Was he a psychopath? Was he insane? Was he a genius? Many prisoners had views about Graham Young. Everyone believed that he could have taught the Russian KGB a thing or two.

Several years later, Graham died from a heart attack. Was it really a heart attack? He could make any mixture to bring on a variety of symptoms.

Some said he was so dangerous that he had to be killed. Others believe that he experimented on himself and it went wrong. Many reckoned that he deliberately topped himself because he knew he would never be released. I think he was messing about with something, probably trying to make a new poison, and he came undone.

Remember, he was never going to get out. It was either high security Parkhurst or Broadmoor again. He was only in his early forties and looked fit enough.

I reckon Graham Young's lethal poison claimed its final victim ...

CHAPTER TWENTY

THE MANY FACES OF PARKHURST

Do you remember the crime of the century? Gold bullion, diamonds and cash worth a grand total of £26 million, or nearly £80 million in today's money, was nicked from a Brink's-Mat warehouse on the Heathrow International Trading Estate in 1983.

There were six robbers who thought they were getting £3 million in cash. They hadn't realise that the sparklers would be in the warehouse, too.

The gang joined the 'faces' with me in Parkhurst. They always clammed up and never admitted it. They were really clever individuals. Admittedly it was evil, pouring petrol on security guards. But the robbers were risking thirty years for that bit of work. On that type of job, onlookers should stand well back.

The name of the game is: if you come onto some robbers when they are on a job, they will 'take you out'.

It's best not to get involved. Insurance companies will pay up. Don't risk your life.

As I said in *I Am Not a Gangster*, a bit of work is a bit of work. It's nothing personal. If I was paid to shoot you I would fucking shoot you, assuming the money was right. It didn't matter if I liked you or didn't like you.

Most people in Parkhurst or Albany would admit after a couple of years that they'd committed the crime. I used to discuss that with Charlie Richardson.

'Most people come clean in the end,' he would say. 'But you must never admit to anything they haven't done you for.'

The Brink's-Mat boys never admitted a thing. Nothing.

When I look back, I remember they were staunch, and that quality was respected. There was a good part to them. When you take people out of crime you see their true self. If those boys had some tobacco and you didn't have any, they would give it to you. If anyone was in the shit, they would help.

I have to mention Charlie Bronson, who is now known as Charles Salvador. Charlie attacked thirty prison officers as well as taking part in ten sieges. They say he caused half-a-million pounds worth of damage with his rooftop protests.

Charlie had a couple of spells at Parkhurst, one of them around the time when I arrived. At one stage, 'C' wing was the only place prepared to take him. Charlie presented Reggie Kray with a pair of boxing gloves, and said he had a 'special bond' with the twins.

I feel very sad for Charlie Bronson. He started off with a seven-year sentence for a botched armed robbery and they electrocuted him – I know what it's like to be electrocuted and doped. Basically they weren't rehabilitating the guy. It was all about brutalisation, and they succeeded in that. They even nutted him off to Broadmoor and Rampton.

Apart from the disorganised armed robbery, all the sentences he received were through his activities in prison. He never killed anyone, and yet he's done more bird than a lifer.

Obviously he was not a well man. Isolation is a very damaging thing. Bronson only ever had a little while on the outside. When you have a dog locked under the stairs and you don't give it any love or any care, don't be surprised that, when you open the door, it bites you.

Yes, Charlie Bronson was a dangerous human being in his Parkhurst days. But they created a monster. Look at what they tried to do to me! Thank God I survived intact.

The Special Security Block at Parkhurst, designed for serial killers, opened in 1966. And it held some absolute monsters. Earlier I told you about Donald Neilson, the Black Panther. There was a serial killer with a similar name, Dennis Nilsen. We talked about his gruesome crimes and plotted to whack him, but we were never allowed anywhere close to him. He came to Parkhurst Special

Security Block in December 1983 after being attacked with a razor blade by an inmate at Wormwood Scrubs.

Nilsen was also known as the Muswell Hill Murderer and the Kindly Killer. The 'kindly' bit was because he believed his style of killing was the most humane you could get. He murdered twelve young men by strangling or drowning them, which was bad enough. After he'd killed them, he bathed and dressed the bodies, then cut them up and flushed the remains down the loo. Sometimes he got rid of the evidence in a bonfire after spending months dismembering the bodies.

And we were only a few walls from Nilsen in the nick! We were all sick when we heard that he had wanked while he looked at the nude, dead bodies. He had some sort of sex with them. Nilsen arranged the corpse of one of the young men on an armchair to watch TV while he enjoyed a boozy night. But he said he never went the whole way, whatever that was supposed to mean. The game was up when a Dyno-Rod employee was called out to investigate blocked drains. The pipes were packed with flesh and bones from Nilsen's victims. They should have hanged the bastard.

There was an armed robber called Rocky, doing seven years. Rocky was an ex-boxer who looked like a seasoned fighter with his flat nose, bashed ears and all that. He was six foot with dark brown eyes and short dark hair. To be fair, he was a good-looking guy despite his war wounds.

Rocky dabbled in cooking for himself and other cons. He knew some of the prisoners who worked in the kitchen, which meant a ready supply of ingredients.

Well, one day Rocky was preparing the evening meal but found that he was short of an onion for his spag bol. He had everything else: mince, spaghetti, Isle of Wight garlic, tomatoes, carrots, bay leaves and parmesan cheese. But he needed an onion. He was working away in a cooking area at Parkhurst when he spotted an onion in a cupboard and added it to the mix.

'Give me back my fucking onion.'

Harry the Cook, who was handy with swords and knives, wasn't going to give up his onion. He looked as if he should give food a rest with his huge gut. Harry the Cook was an imposing blob of a man. But, in a fair fight, he would have stood no chance against Rocky.

Harry the Cook said, in a menacing tone, that Rocky had taken his last onion. Unless he gave it back, the thief would be whacked.

Rocky said Harry was a big baby, and the onion would only make him cry. Harry had been using a knife under supervision while working in the kitchen, but he hadn't returned the blade and sneaked it into his cupboard.

The shiny steel appeared in a flash and became embedded in Rocky's stomach. At the age of forty-one, Rocky was brown bread. And all for the sake of a borrowed onion.

*

Jimmy Davey's original name was Jimmy Beaumont. He changed his name to Davey because his younger brother, Davey, died in police custody. He really hated coppers.

Jimmy was an armed robber who walked with a limp after being shot. He was a Glaswegian, about five-feet-eight, stocky, with dark hair and brown eyes, and was the type of bloke who was always talking about his wife and kids.

This was the man who marked my card, keeping me up to speed with developments, while I arranged the peace treaty between Reggie Kray and Charlie Richardson in Parkhurst. When he got out of prison, he was accused of murdering Paddy Onions, real name Patrick O'Nione, in Tower Bridge Road, London, as part of a gangland feud.

I don't know exactly what happened, but the rumour was that the contract on Paddy was taken out at Parkhurst. It could have been in revenge for a fatal stabbing at a boxing tournament. But the case never went to court because Jimmy also died in police custody shortly after his arrest in 1983. He had to be restrained or some bullshit at a nick in Coventry.

The story made headline news. The inquest was told that Jimmy's legs were tied, his wrists were handcuffed and he was held in a headlock by an officer who weighed sixteen-and-a-half stones.

Well, the huge copper released the headlock when others in the nick noticed that the prisoner had gone blue and stopped breathing.

Doctors switched off Jimmy's life support machine after eleven days.

The jury, in their wisdom, did not agree with the phrase 'unreasonable force'.

You're havin' a laugh, ain't ya? Jimmy's family, their solicitor and the whole of Parkhurst were in a right state about it.

I still haven't got over the verdict of accidental death. As far as I am concerned, justice wasn't seen to be done. But, for me, this was another pointer that I should leave behind my life of crime. So many people were being killed or locked up in jail, with countless lives ruined.

CHAPTER TWENTY-ONE

CHRISTMAS AT PARKHURST

Christmas Eve, 1983. My diary made grim reading, although there was some hope in there, too.

Mum still not well with her leukaemia. She is in and out of hospital. She is still getting lots of drugs. It could take a long time to get better, if she is going to get better. Letter from Vera says Mum could be in remission soon. More tests. Wish I was at home for Christmas. Will dream tonight of log fire, stockings on the mantelpiece and presents in the morning, sing-songs at the table and some good times. Need to read more sociology in case I am accepted for Open University.

I tried to think positively. I was pushing hard to get into the Open University. Charlie Richardson, after his successes with the OU, had recommended me. He had actually written to Maidstone prison, saying I would be a good student at its special education unit. I tried to fill my head with those thoughts and make the most of Christmas Day, four years into a twelve-year sentence.

During the night, the memories I'd had at Kingston returned again – the Queen on the telly, Mum's home-made mice pies and a sneaky glass of sherry.

The build-up to Christmas had been a strange time for us at Parkhurst. At the end of September, thirty-eight IRA prisoners had escaped from Northern Ireland's Maze prison armed with six guns. They hijacked a lorry. A guard died from a heart attack, twenty people were injured and nineteen of the escapees were caught. The IRA men at Parkhurst had been following developments closely, and we watched carefully for their reactions.

Some of the well-known faces were ghosted off to other prisons, and other unfamiliar people filled the cells. Their Irish accents were strong, so they were IRA all right. They kept themselves to themselves a lot during these troubled times, and I watched them standing to attention in their cells.

Then, on 4 December, IRA members Colm McGirr, twenty-three, and nineteen-year-old Brian Campbell were shot dead as they approached an arms dump in County Tyrone. A third man was injured and escaped in a car. The followers on the landing of 'B' wing were downcast, to say the least.

A dark shadow continued to hang over Parkhurst because of more IRA bombings. On 10 December, the IRA set off a bomb at the Royal Artillery Barracks in Woolwich, south London. The blast left a crater, fifteen-feet deep. Three British soldiers were injured.

Another atrocity happened on 17 December, in the afternoon. It was a busy Saturday, and the London streets were filled with Christmas shoppers. A car bomb went off near the side entrance to Harrods, in Hans Crescent. There was a coded message, to the Samaritans, with confusion about the make of car. There was even more confusion when a second call was made, reporting a bomb had been planted at C&A in Oxford Street. That claim proved to be false.

It was carnage, all right, outside Harrods. Three police officers were killed along with three members of the public. Ninety others were hurt including fourteen of the Old Bill. There was damage to five floors of Harrods and twenty-four cars. The street was covered in a shower of glass.

I was shocked at the deaths of so many young people. Most of them were in their twenties. I heard on the news that Denis Thatcher, Margaret's husband, went to the store because 'no damned Irishman was going to stop him'.

The thing that riled me was that the IRA people at Parkhurst were all celebrating, jumping up and down.

'Your mob been at it again?' I groaned as I walked along the landing. I said that a lot of innocent people had been killed – a woman copper who was only twenty-two and also a journalist, only two years older. They just kept celebrating, rubbing their hands with glee.

'They would have had enough warning,' came the reply. I don't think the Parkhurst group knew that there had been a huge balls-up.

The IRA put out a statement saying the Harrods operation was 'not authorised'. IRA people did plant the bomb, but it seems they didn't have permission from HQ.

On Christmas Day itself, the screws came round to unlock the cells and wished us all a happy Christmas. We returned the greetings and went down to breakfast.

It was business as usual for me, with requests for funds to buy a bit of puff. 'Could I borrow a tenner, Bobby, and I'll give it back to you after the New Year?'

Christmas was a sort of amnesty at Parkhurst. The screws left our doors open all day and turned a blind eye to anyone having a bit of puff or a drink of hooch. We went from cell to cell, drinking the hooch, with no fear of retribution. The TV rooms were playing old Christmas films, and some people went there to pass some time. I had a look but, to my horror, 'Merry Xmas Everybody' by Slade was playing on the 1983 *Top of the Pops* show. I'd seen it every year since 1973 and the bloody thing was back in the charts again.

Everybody used to shout: 'We're all banged up, you ponces. Everybody's having fun? Future's only just begun? WE ARE ALL BANGED UP!'

The number of times that telly was ripped off the wall. Honestly, everybody went berserk when the bloody thing came on.

I was touched to receive cards from Mum and my brothers and sisters. I put them up on my table, making a decent display for passers-by to see. I sent out my cards a few days before Christmas to make sure they reached home.

The card from Mum was a treat to read: 'Hope to have you home soon for a Christmas here. Great that you are trying for Open University. You will be the first in our family to go to university.'

I handed out some cards along the landing. I popped into Charlie Richardson's cell. As usual, a book about mining for diamonds was open on his table, alongside a steaming cup of tea. Christmas or not, Charlie was preparing for life on the outside with his obsession to find out more about minerals.

We exchanged greetings and I nipped in to see Reggie. He wasn't so upbeat. I think he was missing Ron, and thoughts of Frances kept returning to him. He put on a brave face of being jovial, although I could see behind it that the very important people in his life were missing. I noticed that he was in the middle of writing to Ron and a couple of other people.

Christmas breakfast was the usual fare but Christmas lunch wasn't bad at all. We had turkey, roast potatoes and Brussels sprouts as well as Christmas pudding and custard. I took the breakfast and lunch back to Charlie's cell, and ate it at his table along with members of his firm who came and went during the day.

The drama on the outside was far from over. On Boxing Day morning, before the cells opened, I listened to the news on my radio. Another bomb had exploded, late on Christmas Day, in Oxford Street. The device had been placed in a bin. Two people, passing by, were taken to hospital with minor injuries. On any other day, the streets would have been packed.

The traditional festive sales were badly hit because of the fear of more bombs. Harrods reopened but lost a small fortune.

The year 1983 was ground-breaking on the outside. *Breakfast Time* was the pioneer morning show on TV; TV-am's *Good Morning Britain* competed on ITV; CDs went on sale in the UK and Pat Jennings, Frankie Fraser's favourite goalkeeper, reached the milestone of 1,000 senior football matches.

New Year arrived and it was quite a happy time. There were no celebrations in Parkhurst on New Year's Eve, but on the day itself we all celebrated that another year, 1983, had gone by.

We saw it as a year under the belt, with less bird to follow. For me, it was a new beginning ...

CHAPTER TWENTY-TWO

THE END OF MY NIGHTMARE

Over the next few months I visited the library as much as possible and attended whatever classes I could. Charlie Richardson provided me with some Open University coursework he'd done, so I tackled some of that.

I also had a few visits from a gentle Buddhist monk called Anju who was promoting his religion and a peaceful existence. He filled in the usual forms and appeared at Parkhurst, offering hope for everyone. Anju was so kind that he made me feel really good. I called him 'skinhead'. I have to say that Anju actually helped to take the violence out of me.

'Bobby, you are going to get out of here,' he predicted. 'Oh yes. Your friend Charlie Richardson is doing the right thing getting you to read the books. I am going to teach you about Buddhism.'

And Anju did teach me about his religion. He was an amazing guy. He looked fascinating, for a start, with his red robe wrapped around him and plain sandals. What a simple outfit. Anju was my spiritual adviser, and allowed to come to my cell. I used to meditate with him.

He said to me, over a jug of mint tea: 'Bobby, try not to act in anger. Always think about negotiating. Take responsibility for your actions. I want you to reform, study and become a better person. You can do this.'

These were encouraging words. He presented me with a book on Buddhism which, he said, would help to control the anger inside me and channel it in another direction – education. If I was upset with the screws, he said, I should just think of them as blue colours and not as the subjects of my wrath. He said I shouldn't see the screws as the Establishment, and blue couldn't hurt me. Anju also encouraged me to write poetry.

> An armour of golden sunlight
> To cover my naked skin
> The power not created by men of war
> But by the love I feel within

Anju loved my poems. His work led to an OBE and a role as spiritual adviser to the King of Thailand.

On a warm, balmy July day in 1984, I stretched out on my bed. I'd had my breakfast and returned to the cell for the brief mid-morning lock-up while the screws had a break.

I heard the familiar clunk of screws' boots coming across the landing. I'd been pretty good recently, I thought, so surely they're not coming to get me? Hold up a minute, the noise from the boots became louder, in the direction of my cell. Here goes, I muttered to myself ...

A couple of young, eager screws opened my cell door. They seemed quite relaxed, not stern-faced, so that had me wondering.

'The Principal Officer wants to see you in the wing office,' one of them said, pointing the way and ushering me out of the cell.

Down the familiar metal staircase, then, to the wing office and I stepped inside. There was a new PO and I didn't know his name. He said he was a McLagan or something Scottish like that.

He stood up as I went into the office. This guy was around five-foot-eightish with brown hair, mid-forties and wearing the customary white shirt and the usual black tie.

'Bobby, I've heard all about you and I can see you've caused a lot of trouble on the outside and the inside.'

'You heard about me taking the Albany governor hostage. It's no secret.'

'Yes, we need to put everything behind you and try for a fresh start. You've behaved yourself for a while now and a few people have been pushing for your education. I can tell you that you've been accepted for the Open University, to study at Maidstone. You need to thank

Charlie Richardson for pushing things, and the new governor at Maidstone.

I was over the fucking moon. 'YES, YES!'

They gave me a minute or two to calm down.

'I know about the education there,' I said when I had collected my thoughts. 'The only problem is, I organised a few sit-downs and caused a lot of havoc in that place a few years ago, so they slung me out.'

'Well, maybe the new Maidstone governor sees some hope for you. He's a good man called Colin Allen. Good luck, son, but don't mess it up this time. If you come back, that'll be it. You'll just stay here. No one else will have you.'

I was off back along the landing like a shot to tell everyone. People were coming out of their cells after the short lock-up and I spread the news like wildfire. I was in a daze as I told Charlie, Reg, Fat Fred Sewell, a couple of oddballs and whoever else was within earshot. I was being given the chance to go to a Category 'B' prison which, I knew, would have a much more relaxed regime.

'Well done, boy,' Charlie shouted. 'You'll soon be as qualified as me.'

Reggie was next: 'I'm sorry to see you go, but I'm glad as well. It's a great opportunity, getting off the island. One day I want to get out of here, too.'

They didn't give me much time to prepare, but I couldn't grumble. They told me one day, and I had to pack my gear the next morning. I was still doing the banking work, and had cash and weapons hidden in my cell, so I had to sort all of that out. I removed the cash from the wall, hid some on my body and left Ian to hand over a lump sum to the new banker. I also handed out blades to trusted chaps. I made sure that I filled in the holes properly, painting them over with the shaving brush and white paint as usual.

I climbed into a prison van again. I was still chained to a screw in the back, but this time it was a much lower security vehicle and didn't look like a mobile Fort Knox arrangement. I could even see properly out of the windows.

As I looked back at Parkhurst, it was like coming out of the Middle Ages and entering a new world. I had spent several years in that gaff and hated the place. It looked like every brick had been built from pain. It was emotional: I was pleased to be leaving the island, but sad to leave my friends behind. Then, when we reached the ferry, I felt as if I was being cleansed.

We arrived in Southampton and I saw people walking around. There was life everywhere, with people going about their business, doing normal things. It felt like winning the lottery and going back to a civilised place.

Going up the motorway it seemed that everything was moving very fast. That was because, in Parkhurst, you walked everywhere and you went from wall to wall. There was no speed and no open spaces. The motorway seemed to me like a racing circuit. I could see a long, road in front of me. I thought of a Hollies song 'He Ain't Heavy,

He's My Brother', with the words: 'It's a long, long road from which there is no return'.

Out of Hampshire and into Kent, I could see greenery, apple trees and so much beauty – things other people take for granted. I felt alive again. I was going into the Garden of England, although it was like entering the Garden of Eden. I had come from a bleak place, oozing with ugliness and brutality, and approaching something beautiful. I felt intoxicated.

I was jolted back in time again when we approached the old stone walls of Maidstone prison. Somehow, though, the 200-year-old surroundings didn't intimidate me, as all I thought about was my Open University course and a route to freedom. We drove through two sets of gates and into the courtyard.

I recognised some of the prison officers at reception: 'Hello, Bobby! Good to see you.'

I returned the greeting, at the same time thinking they were dreading having me back after all the sit-down problems I'd caused ten years earlier. They remembered I'd been there for the manslaughter after I tied the gag too tightly during a robbery. I wondered if they thought: 'Fucking hell, we've got him in here again!'

I was escorted up to Medway wing. After that they decided to put me on Kent wing as it was near the education block. Mind you, that's where I'd caused all the trouble. The governor on Kent wing remembered my sit-down protests and sent me back to Medway.

I was used to doing the prison banking, and I couldn't see anyone who could cope with all the transactions, so I kept it going. I arranged for contacts to smuggle in £50 here and there. I soon built up quite a fund, added to my own smuggled cash, and operated my usual rates of interest. The fixing continued: if anyone needed someone bashed up, I made the call to organise everything. I hadn't gone straight quite yet!

I also had a rude awakening.

'What's that racket? Turn off that shit. Hey, cut out that noise!'

A succession of prisoners yelled across the landing as punk music played, loud headbanging stuff coming from a small speaker. It sounded terrible.

'Switch it off now,' I commanded. 'Put on some Tamla Motown or try Radio 4 for a change.'

Phil the Spy, real name Phil Aldridge, was a punk rocker geezer who had worked in the intelligence service. There he was, all six-foot-plus of him, bopping away in his cell, music blaring, with his black wavy hair also bobbing up and down. Phil was a posh kid whose father worked high up in the military. He tried to sell intelligence to the Russian embassy because he wanted to buy a Mini car. He was about a year-and-a-half into his sentence.

He was one of the youngest people ever to be done for spying. Phil got hold of several pages of partially torn documents, awaiting shredding, while he was working in an intelligence unit in Aldershot. He had to carry information pouches from one place to the other.

The Army rumbled Phil and he was nicked before he could pass on the secrets. Apparently, he had a diary containing notes and telephone numbers of the Soviet embassy. Unfortunately for Phil, he dropped the diary and it was discovered by his commanding officer, who knew that those numbers belonged to the Russians.

It turned out that he had phoned the Soviet embassy several times. Britain was at war with Argentina over the disputed Falkland Islands, and it was believed that the documents included details about the UK's Exocet missiles.

To start with, when MI5 began the investigation, Phil claimed he was trying to see how easy it would be to tap into the Soviet intelligence network. The game was up, though, and details about his wanting to buy the Mini began to emerge. Prime Minister Margaret Thatcher became heavily involved in trying to sort out the mess. There were many reforms in the system after that, and the Security Commission severely criticised lapses in supervision.

But Phil had clearly forgotten all about his spying activities while doing his bird: 'This is today's music,' he shouted. 'Punk is the future of music.'

Phil was a nice kid. I could see why he got his intelligence job, coming from a good military family and with no criminal record. He had a posh accent and he was polite to everyone. He was a bit scatty and naive, like a typical teenager out of a private school.

He wasn't really aware of the real world and the criminality within that world. They threw him in with us lot, so the next thing we were showing him how to get firearms, false passports and documents. Using his potential as an intelligence officer, he could have been an intelligence crook if he'd wanted to be. He saw the other side of the coin in the 'university of crime'.

'Is that quiet enough, Bobby?'

Phil had turned down his record player, so I could just hear some slightly annoying punk sounds.

Phil didn't have my rough, tough background. He was hardly equipped for prison. Of course, he knew what he did was wrong. He was misguided. Imagine wanting to sell state secrets for a Mini. No, Phil was never cut out to be a spy.

'That's fine. Carry on. I can't hear your awful music now.'

The encounter with Phil reminded me of another spy, who I had met during my previous incarceration at Maidstone.

John Vassall was a decent bloke. I could tell that. He was highly educated and intelligent, but fell into a homosexual honeytrap set by the Russians. He didn't seem to be a normal prisoner, with his posh appearance and educated accent.

The Soviet government treated homosexuality as seriously as espionage, so the odds were stacked against our man in Moscow. John was recruited to sell secrets to the Russians during the Cold War years. He was sentenced to eighteen years, and served ten of them.

'I'm going to write a book about my life very soon,' he had told me. 'Listen to my story. I'm going to try to get it published. It was a tragedy for me, but some people will find it juicy, I'm sure, especially with all the sex in Russia. Not that I wanted sex in Russia.'

I'd wondered if it could be John's version of *From Russia with Love*. I decided to keep that thought to myself for the moment. He did write a book about his exploits.

The governor, Colin Allen, took my Open University courses seriously. He provided all of the books I needed and gave me a job as an education orderly. Major Bev Bingham, the chief education officer, supervised me; he shared my views about education and rehabilitation. I could see, from talking to Charlie Richardson, Anju and now Bev, that education was the way forward. I also had thoughts about training ex-offenders for various jobs when they came out, to stop them going back inside again.

Major Bingham also supervised me when I went home to see my mother, who was still seriously ill. Major

Bingham and Colin Allen knew that, if I gave them my word, I wouldn't cause trouble. They let me see my mother without having to wear handcuffs.

Mr Allen had dealt with so many armed robbers. He knew how the criminal mind worked, meaning that he could adapt his regime to cope. If someone played up or went back on their word, he would clamp down. If you played the game, he would respect that and give you a fair deal.

The screws saw that I was being given a chance and they placed bets on me absconding! I was never going to do that – not with the prospect of qualifications and possible employment on the back of everything.

Shortly after my home visit, I was standing on the landing with a pal, Joe Mooney. A screw came up to me, obviously to give some news.

'Your mum is dead.'

I know he was just doing his job, but I didn't like his tone. I told him to fuck off, went back to my cell and cried. I didn't let anyone see me cry.

One of the senior screws let me phone our Vera. 'We were at her side. She went into remission, but then she became very weak and just faded away.'

Mum had lasted four years with the illness, but by 1986 it had really taken hold. I was totally devastated and for a while found it hard to concentrate on anything.

Good old Charlie Richardson sent me a letter, offering condolences about my mum and also wishing me all the best with my courses. He kept repeating the importance of staying out of trouble and keeping my head down.

I received massive support from the Open University tutors. I was disappointed with the screws who specialised in sending my assignments in late. Why did they do that? I think some of them hadn't had a proper education and didn't want to see a con gaining an advantage. The tutors knew what was going on, so none of that counted against me.

The crime aspect of sociology really interested me. Behaviour, seen as deviant by one group, might not be regarded as the same by another group. Rules, established through the generations, can be socially created and not just morally decided. I identified with all of that.

The history of crime echoed from the walls of Maidstone prison. The building, dominated by a four-storey roundhouse, dated back to the early 1800s. All around me, as I studied, I felt that sense of a brutal past. A lot of renovation had gone on, giving buildings a fresh look, although you could see a lot of the original brickwork. It's the prison shown in the title sequence of *Porridge*.

I learned that fifty-eight executions were carried out in the nineteenth century and eleven in the twentieth century. In the earlier years, hangings took place in public outside the main gate.

The busiest man at Maidstone between 1831 and 1872 was the hangman, William Calcraft. He had his craft down to a fine art. During that period, thirty-three people were executed, and there was even a triple hanging. Calcraft killed them all.

I revelled in the studies of sociology and psychology, and I became an Honorary Master of the Open University.

Education? It proved to be my liberation ...

CHAPTER TWENTY-THREE

HARD WORK GOING STRAIGHT

I fell in love at Maidstone prison. It wasn't with a visitor or someone from my previous life. I got together with the prison librarian, Lynn, who had the most amazing eyes and dark brown hair. I had kept a distance from people, not forming close relationships, so this was a major step for me.

It all started when I went to the library to look at the books available, the same as at Parkhurst. When she saw me sitting over there, writing on a piece of paper, asked what I was doing.

'I'm writing poems,' I answered. 'I've organised sit-downs and all that about the way prisoners are treated, but I write poems about it too.'

She really liked my poem about my cell door being locked when I was in Parkhurst.

I have seen dark souls within these walls
Each man's sins made the cross he bore
Yet no darker soul did I ever see
Than the one that locked my door

After she read that and some of my other poems, we felt really connected. The poems inspired her to think even more about how prisoners could be educated and rehabilitated. She was always full of ideas about what courses they could go on.

I was released from Maidstone prison in the summer of 1988. Was this a new beginning? Would I end up back in prison? All of those thoughts filled my head as a hired Rolls-Royce appeared outside the prison gates, reflecting the July sunshine. It seemed to be an announcement to the world that I still had contacts with clout.

Some old friends had clubbed together to hire the limousine. I felt like a lord as Lynn and I glided through the streets of Maidstone towards her idyllic cottage.

Life on the outside seemed weird at first. In prison, all of the decisions are made for you. They organise your activities, tell you when to go for meals and lock you up at bedtime. Here I was, trying to remember what it was like to be independent.

Other ex-prisoners told me how they walked around with bags of change, not knowing how much things cost. A pint of beer in the seventies cost about 20p – now it was more than 90p. A pint of milk was 11p in 1978, doubling in the next ten years.

They were virtually giving eggs away, though, after Health Minister Edwina Currie declared in 1988: 'Most of the egg production in this country, sadly, is now affected with salmonella.'

Christ, it was hard work going straight, especially trying to get a job. I could see on day one that it was essential to educate prisoners, and the public, about the need to prevent re-offending. It would have been so easy to go back to my old ways.

People thought, 'We've got a killer back among us. He's been a hitman and armed robber, banged up at Parkhurst. Best to keep out of his way.'

That was the atmosphere in the late eighties. I was saved, really, by Lynn. We were married at Maidstone Registry Office in the February of 1989. Her mum and dad wouldn't come to the wedding, but her gran, sister and brother joined in. We had a cracking reception at the White Horse pub in East Farleigh near Maidstone.

I got her pregnant, and really needed to find a job. It was almost mission impossible.

As it happened, with my experience as a seasoned armed robber, I had offers of several lucrative bits of work. I could easily have been 'bang at it' again. 'Bobby, it's a good bit of work. It's a nice little earner.' But I was determined to leave my life of crime behind.

Even though I had my Open University qualifications, my prison record went against me. I sent out hundreds of job applications, and some companies obviously didn't even open the envelope. I decided that I was being far too honest about my past.

To be fair, Lynn kept encouraging me. She was adamant, though, that I would turn my back on crime and be there for her and the baby.

'Tell you what I'm going to do,' I said one night as she prepared supper. 'I'm not going to go out into the streets again with Kennedy, but I will have to be a little bit dishonest.'

'What do you mean?'

'I can't get a job by being honest, so I'll have to be dishonest.'

'You're going straight,' she reminded me.

'Okay, I'll report back.'

I just went ahead and did it. I asked my old contacts, not to get me involved in any of their operations, but to suss out companies that had gone under. That way I could add bogus positions to my CV and everything would be difficult to check out.

According to my new CV I was, Operations Manager for Bloggs and Co. or whoever, general builders, until the firm went out of business. Several defunct organisations, unknowingly, helped me to secure future employment. Okay, I became a shelf packer at Tesco on the night shift, but it was a job!

At this stage I could tell that more help was needed for ex-prisoners. I managed to sort out a bank account so I could receive my wages, but I could see this would be tricky for some ex-offenders. Ex-cons don't have a perfect credit history. And more training was definitely required to get reformed offenders into jobs.

All went well at Tesco to start with, putting tins on the shelves. The problem was that I didn't see eye-to-eye with the night manager. In fact, we didn't get on at all. He was only a young kid, maybe about twenty-one, and he strutted around with a folder under his arm, picking fault with everything I did. Now, having been released from prison, I should have avoided the violent option. I was sucked back into my old ways.

I stood there in the aisle, unloading a box, and looked him up and down. He had a round baby face, pink cheeks, long blond hair and looked like Bjorn, the guy from Abba. And he had that bloody folder under his arm.

'You haven't unpacked those dog food tins properly,' he told me with a smirk.

I felt a wave of anger come over me, and said nothing …

I followed the smug geezer into the cold storage area and pushed him up against the wall. I admit that I slapped his face and threatened to hang him up on one of the meat hooks. He looked round at the hooks and I could see he didn't fancy swinging up there with the pig carcasses.

He ran off, and a short while later security staff appeared. They told me to collect my gear and leave the place.

The next morning I came in and was sacked on the spot. I didn't regret what I did to the night manager, and I was thankful that the supermarket hadn't called the Old Bill. I knew, though, that to go straight I would have to channel my energies in a different direction and not threaten anyone else.

In 1990, Lynn and I became the proud parents of our daughter, Sophie. My life had been dark and ugly, and so this frail, beautiful little person meant everything to me. Sophie had gorgeous blonde hair and sensational blue eyes. She looked like her mother apart from my dimple on her chin. The thought of Sophie having to visit me in prison made me even more determined to stay out of trouble.

With my family life appearing stable, I found a job selling advertising space in a local paper, followed by a spell working at a hostel for ex-offenders. I felt more at home there.

My stint as the fixer in Parkhurst meant that I had the skills to take on the role of stock control manager of a cash-and-carry firm in Kent.

It was no secret that I had organised everything in Parkhurst from carefully structured loans to steak and wine for demanding chaps. Also, long before that, in the manor, I had run the day-to-day affairs of a complex operation – and stayed a few steps ahead of the Old Bill for some time. So, to me, the cash-and-carry job was pretty easy.

I could tell from day one that the operation was inefficient. They were losing thousands of pounds by doubling up on things, not following the right procedures and generally making more work for themselves.

'This needs changing, that person shouldn't be doing that, and he needs to keep better records,' I told a senior management geezer and went through a long list.

There was no argument; my changes were brought in.

I kept plugging away with the cash-and-carry company, trying to improve their systems even more, when Lynn became pregnant again. I looked forward to embracing another child and becoming a parent for the second time.

I adored my little Sophie. We couldn't wait for the arrival of the new baby to greet the world in 1992. Mike, my next door neighbour, phoned the cash-and-carry company office to say Lynn had been taken into hospital – good news, you would think.

I dashed home to sort out some things for Lynn and the new baby, assuming that everything was going according to plan. As I arrived home the phone rang.

One of the senior nurses was on the line and told me: 'Your wife needs you, Mr Cummines. Could you come to the hospital straight away?'

The tone of her voice was hardly that of a nurse about to welcome a new baby into the world. I rang a taxi and prepared to speed off to the hospital.

When I arrived, I was ushered into a private room. Lynn's face told me everything. I knew then that the baby was dead. Lynn, weeping, whispered that our girl was in the hospital chapel, so I left my wife and followed the signs. As I opened the door I noticed a small wicker basket. Inside the basket, the perfect little baby. I just cried and cried. I saw a little girl. A lifeless little girl.

My pride and joy, precious playmate for my gorgeous Sophie, would have been called Abigail.

Lynn and I cried for weeks. It was such a feeling of helplessness, not even being to say hello to my new daughter.

Sadly, the marriage to Lynn didn't last, but my daughter Sophie became the jewel of my life.

I continued to move from job to job, usually sorting out logistics problems, but that wasn't enough. I had to find more ways of channelling all of that energy, built up over the years, including during my stretch in Parkhurst. I had used it in an aggressive and violent way for such a long time; now I needed to harness all of that energy and push hard to help ex-offenders.

My old probation officer at Maidstone, Maurice, told me about Mark Leech. A former prisoner, Mark was setting up a charity run by ex-offenders for ex-offenders.

Mark had caused problems in prison; he was a difficult customer for the authorities to deal with. He was well educated, had an answer for everything, and tied them in knots with his legal knowledge. He was working on a scheme to help ex-offenders lead a normal life in

Civvy Street. Mark's ideas on training, rehabilitation and counselling matched my thoughts exactly.

We started Unlock in my garage with £6. We could see that it was difficult for former prisoners to get into work, so I thought: how can we help these people? I knew there were lots of good charities trying to help, but they didn't understand the culture of ex-offenders. They had read about it but hadn't lived it.

For someone out of work and struggling, the drug-dealer's proposition would be attractive: 'You don't have to suffer. Work for me, help with my business and I will give you £500 a week in your hand. It's easy money.'

So the system geared them up to fail and return to criminality. At least in the criminal environment they were respected and earned cash. They could go out and buy new trainers and the latest gadgets. And they were popular people; I was also popular during my crime years, but I was still banged up for a long time.

I saw that, when ex-prisoners were excluded from society, with a constant millstone of a criminal record round their neck, people treated them like dirt. So drug-dealing, criminality and burglary appeared to be the best options.

Reformed offenders carried their sentences and criminal records round with them. They were sentenced twice. They were sentenced in the courts and served that time; then the criminal records check meant that they couldn't get a job and were prevented from integrating back into society.

As a charity, we were 'real' to our people. Unlock was about stopping social exclusion and trying to break down the barriers of employment, health and finance – bringing ex-offenders back into society so that they could become taxpayers rather than a burden on taxpayers. It was all about equality and stopping social exclusion.

We started setting up bank accounts for reformed offenders. Employers now paid using the BACS system, so it wasn't practical to employ someone who could only accept cash in hand.

There was also the issue of insurance for former prisoners. The family of an ex-inmate might have no criminal records. But if an ex-offender moved into their house, the home contents and buildings insurance would be void immediately. And so people didn't want members of their family staying with them because their home would have been at risk. We went to see Lloyd's underwriters and managed to get sixteen brokers to service affected families.

Companies were finding that reformed offenders made excellent employees. The former prisoners knew how hard it was to get a job, so they normally stayed with the employer who gave them the first chance. If there was a fiddle going on in the company, they were often the first to spot it and find ways of preventing future abuse. They didn't want to be accused of anything!

Many media interviews came our way through Unlock. From 2000 onwards, I was a familiar face on Sky, ITV and the BBC, and radio listeners got used to hearing about the organisation. I was on a mission to bring about huge changes and bring ex-offenders back into society.

I am proud to say that, since Unlock started, the organisation helped hundreds of ex-offenders to go on training schemes and to find employment.

I welcomed a distinguished visitor to the Unlock office in Snodland, Kent. Who else but Norman Parker, who experienced the worst of Parkhurst a few years before me?

First, he served six years for manslaughter – in 1963, aged eighteen, he shot his Nazi girlfriend because he thought she was about to shoot him. Then in 1971, he was convicted of a gangland killing. He spent twenty-eight years in more than twenty jails. Norman was moved around from prison to prison, including Parkhurst. This was our first ever meeting.

Norman had a reputation for being staunch and always in the thick of things. If there was a riot or hunger strike, even an escape attempt, then Norman would have something to do with it. He had also encountered people like the Krays and the Great Train Robbers in various prisons, so we had plenty to talk about.

To serve a long sentence like that, Norman said, a prisoner needs amazing strength, determination and tenacity. He shared my memories of brutality by some of the prison officers. He remembered an incredibly savage regime in Parkhurst. His own book, *Parkhurst Tales*, was written to show the public what really happened. He said he faced such brutality that the only weapon in his armoury was the ability to fight back. He felt that, in his day, the screws were not supervised enough – and the system brutalised them as well as the prisoners. That meant that some of the prison officers were allowed to do what they wanted and get away with atrocious behaviour in the seventies and eighties.

Norman followed the same path as me through the Open University and obtained an honours degree. He studied hard and gained a master's in criminology from the University of Surrey.

We had a brilliant chat about rehabilitation, the importance of training schemes and, of course, the bad old days in Parkhurst.

'We've got another special visitor coming to see us today,' I told Mark one morning as we prepared to go into the Unlock office.

'Oh, who's that then?' he asked, taking a keen interest as usual.

A knock at the office door, a firm handshake, coffee on the stove and I was soon talking about old times.

Paddy Joe Hill still looked in good shape, fit and wiry, but he had fire in his eyes. He still had anger in his voice about the treatment of the Birmingham Six, despite the fact that the convictions had been quashed. He wanted a lot more.

'I didn't do it and I want them to admit what they did. I went to so many nicks in solitary after being fitted up.

I should have a Queen's Pardon and so should all of us. The public need to know, for sure, that the police were bent. They need to know all of the facts.'

'I remember when I first saw you in Parkhurst. I knew you'd been fitted up,' I told him. 'You kept going on about it, for a start!'

Paddy and the other five had been a neat fit for the crime. Because I was living with the IRA in the late seventies and early eighties, I knew he didn't speak their political language. Of course, he had form, but he was not a bomber.

Paddy had some observations to make on Unlock: 'One thing I can see about your operation here. There are too many straightgoers. They don't know how to deal with ex-offenders. If someone hasn't been to jail and experienced everything there, they won't know what's needed to help people reform.'

Sadly, around 2000, Mark's health deteriorated. He thought it best to stand down and hand the organisation – which was flourishing with five staff and four volunteers – over to me. Sir Stephen Tumim, the judge who had been a critical Inspector of Prisons, was our first president, and after he died, Sir David Ramsbotham stepped in. Judge John Samuels acted as vice president. Chief executive was a challenging role for me but I put everything into it, and I was pleased to receive backing from people in high places.

I was invited to sit on many government think-tanks and committees. I was appointed specialist advisor to the

House of Commons Home Affairs Committee on the Rehabilitation of Offenders Act, chaired by John Denham, MP. I was also a member of the Deputy Prime Minister's Advisory Committee.

Anyone who's been following the dramatic highs and lows of my life will know that, on Monday, 11 July 2011, I received the OBE from the Queen. The announcement at Buckingham Palace said that I was receiving the award for my work with reformed offenders.

I bowed before the Queen, as she pinned the medal on my left lapel, and I simply said: 'Thank you, ma'am.'

Her Majesty told me: 'You have a very colourful background.'

Colourful? That was probably the understatement of the century.

I met the love of my life, Ami, in a nightclub in the mid-nineties. She had lived in Newcastle for a while and it was unusual to hear a Japanese bird talking with a Geordie accent. We became good friends and, after a few weeks of chatting, I invited Ami and her son Kai to visit me in Kent. We spent Christmas together and things moved on from there.

We were married at the Archbishop's Palace in Maidstone. Close friends and family attended the service, followed by the reception at a nearby inn, overlooking the River Medway.

Naturally, Ami's family were worried that I might still by carrying out bits of work like armed robberies. I was able to show them that I had reformed with my charity work and they could see what I was doing. I did chuckle, knowing that I had been accused of stealing the Japanese Instrument of Surrender, and now here I was with a Japanese wife!

CHAPTER TWENTY-FOUR

FAREWELL TO
THE KRAYS

I was devastated to hear about the deaths of Reg and Ron Kray. Obviously, I was much closer to Reg because we lived and breathed in Parkhurst together.

The first to go was Ronnie, who died in hospital at the age of sixty-one on 17 March 1995. He was in Broadmoor at the time, and was suffering from anaemia and exhaustion. He was taken to Heatherwood Hospital in Ascot. I had no idea that his life was at risk because at worst, I heard, he had a bleeding ulcer.

Well, he was treated and returned to Broadmoor but still said he didn't feel right. He was taken to Wexham Park Hospital in Slough where he died from a heart attack. I knew that he was always pumped full of drugs, adding to his habit of about a hundred cigarettes a day.

As soon as I heard the news, I got a message of condolence through to Maidstone prison. Reg had been moved to the Weald wing there in March 1994. I knew someone who was doing bird there, so I preferred to pass the message through him rather than letting a screw give my sympathies to Reggie. I just sent a message saying my thoughts were with Reggie and family at a tragic time. Loyal Krays' supporter Freddie Foreman was in Maidstone as well with Reggie, so he was there to give some comfort.

I knew what the funeral was going to be like, so I refused to attend. I didn't want to go along and see people who had never even met the twins. The entire event was turned into a carnival. It should have just involved those who loved Ronnie and were closest to him. As it turned out, every Tom, Dick and Harry wanted to be at St Matthew's Church, just round the corner from the family home in Vallance Road. I saw the pictures of a Victorian-style black hearse with six plumed black horses leading the procession.

Reggie was allowed out of prison for the first time in twenty-seven years, and I thought it was all a bit much for him. I saw that his prison car was mobbed as it set off along Bethnal Green Road. Ron and Reg would both have wanted the big show, but not from geezers who were just there for the sake of being seen. It's the same as when any famous person dies: you have people laying flowers and everything, but some of them have never even met the person.

My way of showing respect was to remember the things they did for me and my mum, like sending flowers and paintings when she was ill. Ron and Reg did some terrible things. But so did I, and I have to put myself in that frame. However, in our world, when there is a death or tragedy, the humanity comes out and we are there for each other.

Fast forward then to 1 October 2000, when Reggie passed away. He had cancer and was allowed out of prison in the August of that year because of his poor health. He died in the honeymoon suite of the Beefeater Town House Hotel in Norwich. By his side were his wife Roberta, Freddie Foreman and his old pal Jerry Powell. Reg wanted to listen to music and look out over the river in his final days.

I received a phone call, shortly after Reggie died.

'Reggie has gone,' was all the caller said.

I said a very brief 'thank you'. There was nothing else to say. I knew how ill he had been. I thought to myself that none of us were getting any younger. We were used to seeing friends and relatives at christenings and weddings, but recently I had been meeting those same people at funerals.

'Another part of our history is gone,' I said to myself.

Reg died in the arms of Freddie Foreman. He was semi-conscious and struggling to breathe.

'Don't fight it, let it go,' Freddie told him. 'See you another time, another place.'

Three years earlier Reggie had married Roberta Jones, who was an English graduate. They were married in the chapel at Maidstone prison on Monday, 14 July 1997. The prison walls were lit up on the eve of the wedding by a laser show, which was typical of Reggie. After the ceremony the prison authorities allowed a two-hour, alcohol-free reception. Over the road, at a nearby pub, other friends and relatives gathered to have a celebration, too.

It was an unusual marriage because Roberta was more intrigued by Reggie than anything else. She couldn't get her head around how he managed to stay sane after all that time in prison. Roberta was certainly committed to him and campaigned hard for his release. It was his second marriage, of course, because his first wife Frances killed herself way back in 1967.

I remembered having cups of tea with Reggie, and enjoying our little chats. I recalled his ideas for a mafia-style operation in England and how he wanted to buy that big house with plenty of land. He always planned to enjoy that reality with Ron.

You could have a good laugh with Reg. You had to tell your joke close to his ear because of his slight deafness. He might not hear you first time, but then he would understand you properly and have a really good laugh, cracking his own jokes.

People who really knew Reggie saw the other side. If you were out of teabags in the nick, he would get some for you. If you were out of tobacco or anything else, he would share. He even helped out the nutters and loons. He would smoke a cigarette halfway down and give the rest of it to the lunatics or people who had lost their way, who went around looking for butts. In among the violence and everything else, there was that other side to Reg.

When my mum died, Reg had a musical box made by Fat Fred in the nick, and sent it to the family along with bunches of flowers. He would hear something on the telly, say about a kid having leukaemia, and he would sell some of his paintings to send a few quid the child's way. I saw that sort of thing happen a lot.

I lived on the landing with Reg twenty-four hours a day, seven days a week, fifty-two weeks a year. So I knew when he was up, when he was down, worried about Ron or had something else on his mind. At certain times of the year he would think about his mum or his first wife Frances who died all those years before I met him. Like everyone else, Reggie was in a world of his own in there. The only people who really knew Reg and Ron were those who worked with them or did bird at the same time – everyone else is just guessing.

Reggie never had to go about 'giving it large' because he had the respect and reputation. He didn't have to do all that. There aren't too many people who did time with Reggie and had a bad word to say about him. If you messed with Reg or tried to take a liberty with him, then he would deal with it – and deal with you rather rapidly. But if he could do you a favour, he would do you a favour.

The screws just left Reggie to do as he liked – they left most of us alone, really. The only ones they watched carefully were the nutcases. Reggie, like everyone else, was just keen to get on with his bird and look for a way out.

I didn't go to Reg's funeral either. Again, the plumed horses appeared along with that massive show of loyalty. Once more, though, I felt it was all too much and over the top. The hearse had 'REG' in huge letters. Frank Sinatra's 'My Way' echoed in St Matthew's Church as Reggie was reunited with Ronnie.

I went along to the church when it was quieter to pay my own respects. I felt emptiness while I was sitting there with my memories. I thought that, if some wanted to go to a big show, they could go to a rock concert. I sat there with a candle and paid my respects that way. Reg had religion in him as well – he believed in God.

I was really sad to hear about the death of the eldest Kray brother, Charlie, at the age of seventy-three. He was affable and good company. His passing, in the same year as Reggie, meant that all three Krays spent their final years in prison.

He suffered chest pains at Parkhurst and was taken to St Mary's Hospital on the Isle of Wight, where he passed away with close family at his bedside.

Charlie was in Parkhurst after being caught up in a drugs-smuggling operation. He acted as an agent for the twins, booking acts at their nightclubs and bars. He was involved with Krayleigh Enterprises, offering bodyguards and security. Frank Sinatra was said to be a client, showing the power of the Krays – even when the twins were behind bars.

I will always remember Charlie Kray as a gentle man, who inevitably lived in the shadow of his brothers. When the twins were in trouble, they turned to Charlie, and his life was always mapped out in front of him.

I say to Reggie, Ronnie and Charlie Kray: R.I.P., my friends.

CHAPTER TWENTY-FIVE

FAREWELL TO CHARLIE RICHARDSON

Charlie Richardson was my best friend, in and out of prison. Without his words of encouragement and insistence on my Open University courses, I would have been back on the streets with a shotgun.

Only a week or two before he died, I popped in to see Charlie, his wife Ronnie and the kids. He was sitting in his front room, perched on his old leather armchair as usual. He had been released in 1984, after serving seventeen years of his twenty-five-year sentence.

'Promise me you'll look after Ronnie and these kids if anything happens to me. If something does happen, you know that the vultures will fly.'

'Yes, of course I'll look after them,' I answered, realising that he knew more than he was saying, but not intending to alarm me or make a fuss.

Not long afterwards, I decided to treat Charlie to a meal out. There was no particular occasion; I just thought he deserved it because of everything he'd done for me.

I went along to his house with Joe, a friend of many years standing, and picked up Charlie and Ronnie at around eleven o'clock in the morning. My idea was to take them for a slap-up lunch to show my gratitude for his support in and out of prison.

I arrived in my blue Jag. Charlie loved that motor with its classy lines and plush upholstery. He suggested a nice little restaurant, not far from his village in Kent.

'What do you want to eat?' I asked when we got there, knowing I had more than just a few quid in my pocket. 'You can have anything you like.'

'I'd love a lobster thermidor,' Charlie answered, with that familiar twinkle in his eye.

'I'll have the same please,' Ronnie beamed while Joe and I plumped for the steaks.

What a meal it was. I made sure we had plenty of champagne and the bill reflected our indulgence! I paid the waiter in cash without any problem, as I had built up funds with my legit earnings over the years. He was a bit taken aback, probably expecting plastic, and he received a decent tip, too.

We all went back to Charlie's house, where the main man produced his usual olives and cheese as well as a drop of white wine. He put the world to rights, as he normally did. This was a normal day for us with his two huge black dogs, like wolves, running about. Charlie had a habit of dipping a biscuit in his wine to wind up Ronnie. He performed his usual trick, Ronnie complained, and we all had a good laugh.

A few nights later, on 19 September 2012, the phone rang. I was standing in the kitchen with my wife, Ami. She was cooking the tea. It was Ronnie on the phone.

'Charlie's gone,' was all she said.

I thought he had got up to some mischief and was on his toes, making himself scarce.

'Ronnie? What do you mean he's gone?'

'He's died.'

It was like someone had punched a hole in my chest and ripped my heart out. Charlie had complained of feeling unwell. He was taken to hospital and died shortly afterwards from peritonitis.

Ami said to me: 'I've seen you after a few of your friends have died, but it's the first time I've watched you cry.'

I was in bits for a while. I went for a walk and tried to get it all in my head. I couldn't help thinking that I had been round their house just the other day and he'd been to my wife's birthday party. It wasn't as if he was lingering on in hospital – it just happened too quickly. I wanted to be on my own.

I wasn't much help to Charlie's family for a day or two, and then I was there for them to make the funeral arrangements. One thing we decided was that it wouldn't be a carnival, like the twins' funerals. It was going to be a respectful send-off for our Charlie.

More than 200 people attended the funeral service at Honor Oak Crematorium in south London on 8 October 2012.

Ronnie Richardson handled all the arrangements, including flowers and invitations, while I looked after security. I wouldn't allow any photographs apart from those taken by the official photographer.

Floral tributes were taken to Brenchley Gardens cemetery. Charlie's mother Eileen and brother Alan are buried there. Dulwich Hamlet Football Club, with strong links to the Richardsons, was the venue for a gathering of friends and family. When I saw the coffin with his little hat on top, it threw me for a few seconds.

I said in my eulogy that, on the day Charlie died, it really knocked me for six. I said that, without his words of wisdom, I would have rotted in prison, gone back into crime or ended up on a pavement with a bullet in my back. In my manor, there would have been people ready to topple me and take my place. No doubt that was a possibility for the Krays, too, if they'd gone back to their old territory.

There will never be another Charlie Richardson.

CHAPTER TWENTY-SIX

MY MISSION

I became disillusioned with the way Unlock was operating – and decided to leave in 2012.

People reported back to me that the project didn't seem to be moving forward the way I had intended, just as Paddy Joe Hill predicted. When I was there, I tried to get things done. As well as obtaining bank accounts and securing insurance for ex-prisoners, I became involved in training schemes.

One company, Phoenix Training Services in the Midlands, was run by someone who didn't know much about ex-offenders. He soon learned. They started offering schemes like forklift-driving courses to get our people back into work.

So, yes, I was the kid on the block, doing it, but I believed that Unlock and similar groups were going through the motions and ticking the right boxes, without living in the real world. I saw that some charities were not making much difference, just churning out glossy literature.

People said I had changed a lot of lives, and I couldn't just walk away from the business of rehabilitation. I thought about it and had a look at what was going on. Someone had to go out and meet the offenders and their families to make progress.

I decided in 2016 to start an organisation called Advantage for Disadvantaged People. I want to build on the work Unlock did for ex-offenders by pushing for training schemes and improving job prospects, but this is not just for ex-offenders; this is across the board. For example, we also have soldiers coming back from war zones, suffering from post-traumatic stress and not getting the help they need. They miss the camaraderie of the forces and feel that they have been thrown on the scrapheap.

'I missed my mates, Bobby,' one told me. 'I went through hell with the stress from the bombs and shootings, and it seemed to me that people didn't care. I started drinking a lot and got into drugs. There was a dealer in the pub, and he probably saw that I was vulnerable. Anyway, the drugs were cheap to start with, and then I had to steal to pay for them. I was caught doing a burglary. It feels like the end of the road for me.'

That case is typical, but it is far from the end of the road. There are so many former squaddies like that. My job is to talk to the military and training companies, find out what is being done and how the situation can be improved.

I am looking at every group that is discriminated against. I am going round, checking on all the training and support agencies, monitoring them to see that they are doing what they say they are doing. Otherwise, they are just copping money for not doing enough to help. The aim is to get more and more people to become law-abiding, contributing members of our society.

When I say 'across the board' for my new scheme, it means exactly that. I am looking at anyone who is living with a disadvantage. We need to help single parents who are struggling. Young mums find themselves with a little baby and they can't go to work. They are looking for someone to look after the baby, but have no support.

What about people in wheelchairs? Those who are dyslexic? Adults who have never had a formal education?

All of these groups are costing the taxpayer millions of pounds every year. I want them to learn a proper trade, where possible, or receive the best help and advice available to reach their full potential. They need not be a burden to the taxpayer; they can play active roles in our society, with the correct advice and encouragement.

Advantage for Disadvantaged People also concentrates on kids who are not in trouble yet, but could easily go down that route. We try to get them before they arrive in prison, not when they are inside with a criminal record.

We talk to families. Some children are going back to the same nonsense all the time at home. Many of the parents I meet are law abiding citizens, but in other cases criminality can be traced back to the home, so I work with mums and dads from all backgrounds.

When a kid gets into trouble I have parents on the phone, crying, asking what is it like to go to court? What is it going to be like in prison? The parents might have watched American TV where someone was raped in jail and people received ninety-nine-year sentences. Well, none of that happens in the UK, of course, but parents do write to me with their concerns.

A typical letter reads: 'Our son has to go to court, and he hasn't been in trouble before. We're worried sick. Can you help? Can he get parole? Will he never get a job?'

Now, I can help in several ways. I explain how the legal process works. Half of the people who write to me have never even been inside a police station, let alone a cell. If someone looks like receiving a custodial sentence, I sit everyone down and explain what will happen. I explain to the offender what to expect, how to behave in prison and what to avoid. I show how to get released early, as well as how not to get involved in nonsense, prison politics and violence.

If a mum is going to prison, the kids are likely to go into care. If the dad goes into jail, the mum is struggling to visit him and bring up the kids properly. When the kids go to school, they are taunted about their mum or dad being in prison – so the children are discriminated against.

Recently I've been visiting schools to warn children against carrying guns and knives. I've also been explaining the menace of drugs. I've been going into classrooms, telling the kids straight.

I impress on them the fact that a lot of gear is not pure. Drugs dealers could not care less what is in their lethal packets. All sorts of pollutants can be in there such as detergents and laxatives. I've even heard of lead being used to make a drug heavier.

Some of the kids I talk to in schools are already carrying knives. I explain to them that 'mugs take drugs and fools carry tools'.

I ask: 'Do you know that someone carrying a weapon is thirty-three times more likely to be a victim of violent crime?'

They don't know that figure, and they also don't realise that, when a geezer is cut up, his girlfriend will probably get the same treatment. That is just the way things happen on the streets.

Another key message is that when people come looking for someone, the other person will be carrying a weapon as well. That seems to make them think, with the prospect of an evil guy cutting and slashing at them. The kids sit up and take notice of everything; I can only hope that they spread the messages.

New proposals to deal with knife crime are designed to act as a deterrent. Personally, I think extra resources should be used in schools to nip the problem in the bud.

Police in England and Wales say there were 29,000 crimes involving knives in the year up to March 2016. That is a 10 per cent rise on the previous year. The Sentencing Council for England and Wales wants to clamp down on offenders because of the devastation caused to victims and their families. That will mean much longer sentences for people carrying knives. It is disturbing that possession of knives or bladed weapons rose 16 per cent to 11,500 in a year.

Sentences were handed out to 7,800 adults and 1,400 young offenders in that year. Surely many of them could be persuaded to take a different path in life?

Prison is about revenge at the moment, rather than helping people back into society. I let friends and families know that I am pushing for more education before the crimes are committed, and rehabilitation afterwards, rather than keeping that cell door firmly shut.

I feel that I have emerged from the darkness and into the light. I've committed some horrible crimes. I've survived Britain's Alcatraz and it has helped me to see where I went wrong, and how to prevent other people from taking the same route. Yes, I believe that I can make a difference. A real difference in the real world.

For the record, the name Parkhurst was lost in 2008. The two other prison names, Albany and Camp Hill, were dispensed with too. The new 'super prison' is called HMP Isle of Wight, with Camp Hill eventually closing altogether.

The high security status of my day has gone; now HMP Isle of Wight is a Category 'B' male training prison. The place holds around 1,100 prisoners on two sites, and they're mainly sex offenders. A third of them are serving life sentences, or jail terms with no definite end date, to protect the public.

There's more emphasis now on relationships between staff and prisoners, and concentrating on the worth of a person. Charlie Richardson, with his communication skills, would have been a top man arranging any of that. Charlie campaigned on behalf of young offenders after he was released, and he was always trying to find ways of getting young offenders into education and out of prison. He managed all of that at the same time as pursuing his legitimate business ideas, such as mining interests and even organising blazers for Ugandan athletes at the 1988 Seoul Olympics!

There is no place now for revenge. The way ahead is rehabilitation and, if I can play any part in that transformation, then I am ready and waiting.

And, thank God, the likes of Parkhurst and Albany will never be allowed to flourish again. From the depths of despair, we can only hope that a brighter future lies ahead in the prison system. I survived my years at Parkhurst; thank God those days are gone. For ever.

ACKNOWLEDGEMENTS

Charlie Richardson, R.I.P.; Ronnie Richardson and her kids; Noel 'Razor' Smith; Professor Dick Hobbs; Fred Dinenage; my co-writer David Meikle; Joe Baden and family; Norman Parker; Andy, Mel and family; Mark, Lily and family; David Mais; Chris Lloyd, Yvonne and family; Mark Lucas; Paul Stone; Giuseppe and family; Kate, Matt and family; my brother Jack and family; Colin Cook; Coutts Bank; the Open University; the politicians and judges who believed in me; and all of my family everywhere.

ABOUT THE AUTHOR

At sixteen, Bobby Cummines became one of the youngest people in Britain to be convicted of carrying a sawn-off shotgun. He quickly became a gangland leader and was convicted of a number of serious offences including manslaughter and bank robbery. After serving twelve years in many of the UK's maximum security prisons, he went on to become a founder member and chief executive of Unlock, a charity which helps people with criminal convictions reintegrate into society. He is also a co-founder of Midas which helps young people from disadvantaged backgrounds. In 2011 he was an awarded an OBE.

Bobby is one of the UK's leading penal reformers and has advised Ministers and Judges as well as public and private sector agencies on prison and rehabilitation. His passion is talking to young people in schools and colleges, deterring them from what they might perceive as a glamorous lifestyle by highlighting the harsh realities of crime and prison.